Junior Lawyers' Handbook

Other titles available from Law Society Publishing:

Career Management for Lawyers: Practical Strategies to Plan Your Next Chapter
Rachel Brushfield

Legal Training Toolkit
Melissa Hardee

Titles from Law Society Publishing can be ordered from all good bookshops or direct (telephone 0370 850 1422, or visit our online shop at **www.lawsociety.org.uk/bookshop**).

Junior Lawyers' Handbook

How to Navigate the Transition from Student to Legal Professional

Eloise Skinner

The Law Society

ISBN-13: 978-1-78446-130-0

Published in 2019 by the Law Society
113 Chancery Lane, London WC2A 1PL

Typeset by Columns XML Design Ltd, Reading
Printed by Hobbs the Printers Ltd, Totton, Hants

FSC
www.fsc.org
MIX
Paper from responsible sources
FSC® C020438

The paper used for the text pages of this book is FSC® certified. FSC (the Forest Stewardship Council®) is an international network to promote responsible management of the world's forests.

'Inspiration will have advance, affirmation, the forward foot, the ascending state; it will be an opener of doors.'

– Ralph Waldo Emerson

***

With thanks to Beth, Georgia, Hannah, Raj, Greg, and Christa – your guidance and wisdom has been invaluable.

Contents

About this book

Firstly, congratulations! After all those years of interviews and application forms – you've made it. You've got your foot in the door and your name firmly printed on your very own training contract. You've proved yourself, sat all of your exams, and updated your LinkedIn title. This book is about what comes next.

The transition to becoming a junior lawyer can be daunting. Not only are you faced with a new professional environment, a new pace of life and a whole cohort of new colleagues, but the world around you is changing fast. Old structures are evolving; diversity and social mobility are shaking up former hierarchies; technology is revolutionising the profession. Add to this the increasing speed and competition in the market, and it's fair to say that today's junior lawyers are facing unprecedented challenges as they enter the workplace.

If you're reading this book, chances are you're interested in your own development during this crucial period of transition. You want to be ahead of the game, firmly on the path to growth, and building the foundations that will shape the basis of your future career. As you begin any new job, professional and personal skills are often overlooked in favour of technical expertise. This is great for learning how to do – with competence – the work for which you're paid, but not so great when it comes to building the toolkit of skills you'll take with you throughout your career (and life). This was where I found myself, starting out as a junior lawyer, wondering why it was so difficult to find an up-to-date, practical, comprehensive resource to help me move forwards with confidence.

And so, I set out to find a solution. I wanted to create something that would provide structure and form to the rapid personal and professional change that takes place during the first stages of your career. Something that you can flick through and refer back to and make notes in and pass on to a friend. Most importantly, I wanted to produce something that meets you on your level, where you are, and speaks to you in a language that is not only relevant but – I hope! – genuinely interesting.

Of course, I didn't just want to offer you my experience. I spent months gathering material from the experts – industry leaders and those at the top of their game – as well as sourcing feedback from the people who recently experienced the transition themselves. In other words, people who were just like you. I've distilled this wisdom and experience in the pages of this book.

The advice and guidance that follows isn't groundbreaking, or overly complex. What it is, however, is effective. Very few junior lawyers go to the effort to constantly plan, track and manage their own skillset and career during the training contract years. Putting in the effort at an early stage will set you apart from others, build up your portfolio of transferable skills, and train you in flexibility, adaptability and self-awareness. Most importantly, it will give you the clarity to see the road ahead, during a period where your career – and your personal skillset – can seem uncertain.

This book is also driven by a deep belief that this period of your new legal career, in its very earliest stages, should be exciting. It should be a steep learning curve, yes – but it should also be a new adventure into the professional world, with all of its accompanying challenges and rewards. In short, you should enjoy it. However – speaking from experience – it's difficult to find the enjoyment, interest and passion in the work when you feel like things are out of control; when you feel like work is chaotic and you're falling behind. That's where this book comes in.

In the pages that follow, you'll find advice, guidance and wisdom from those who have walked the same path before (and survived!). Filled with actionable, practical tips, this book will not only teach you how to get through the working day with ease, but also how to genuinely add value, stand out from the crowd and map your future career with confidence.

It's important to emphasise one thing from the start: there is no single perfect way of becoming an outstanding junior lawyer. The advice gathered in this book is just that – advice – and it is not intended to be prescriptive. Think of this book less as a step-by-step instruction manual and more as a portfolio of tools for you to integrate into your working life, as and when it suits you best.

Entering the legal world is not a step to be underestimated: you're joining a profession with centuries of establishment, in the midst of massive disruption. As a junior lawyer at this time in history, you'll be directly involved in shaping and forming the legal industry of the future. It's an exciting time, and it's important work. This book is here to help you make the most of your time as a junior lawyer, at the very start of the journey.

It's often been said that thoughts and intentions don't become reality until you start putting them into action. I encourage you to be playful, curious and proactive as you build your career foundations, and you may find that making notes on the process helps you to experience the transition with more awareness and clarity.

Essentially, this is the book I wish I'd had in my own transition from university graduate to starting out as a junior lawyer. I hope you find it as helpful as I would have done (and still do!). And – finally – as you begin to build the foundations of your legal career, I hope that you can find fulfilment in the journey itself, wherever it takes you.

Chapter 1

Communication: the written word

Crafting correspondence for the business world

This chapter will introduce you to the art of business writing. In the following pages, you'll learn how to deliver actionable, clear correspondence, and craft a message that will make your emails stand out within your recipient's overflowing inbox. You'll work on shaping your tone, voice and language to reflect the context, and – with a bit of luck – you'll even learn to write something that makes someone's Monday morning a little more joyful.

What's your point?

The first rule of business writing is this: make a point, and make it clearly, quickly and effectively. This is not the time for academic writing, where your professors were paid to spend long hours immersing themselves in your thoughts. At work, your supervisor is going to want to know the conclusion as soon as possible.

With this in mind, start your written work with the answer to the question you've been asked, and not the one you *wish* you'd been asked. You'll get bonus points if you add in a recommendation, immediate action plan or suggestion for next steps in order to proactively move the project forwards.

Crafting correspondence

It's one thing to send off an email that meets your supervisor's expectations and gets the job done. It's another thing entirely to develop correspondence that makes a point with accuracy and distinction. It's one thing to manage to elicit a response; it's another thing to actively advance an exchange and deliver an email that your recipient actually wants to read. Here are a few pointers on writing with professional excellence.

Consider your tone

If you've had previous correspondence with the recipient, see if you can reflect their style within your own draft. Are they direct and brief in their emails, or do they prefer formalities? Which phrases have they used to open and close the correspondence? Do they use bullet points or paragraphs of text? Are they light-hearted or controlled in speech? Most importantly, can you incorporate any subtle elements of their own communication in your response?

It's also worth bearing in mind that communicating with different jurisdictions will require a sensitivity to different cultural formalities.

Offer to help out

This principle applies even if you have offered every single time, and they've never taken you up on it. It applies even if your instinct (and deepest desire) is not to offer. It applies internally (to colleagues, supervisors and partners), and externally (to clients, regulators and anyone else you come across).

The point is to establish a relationship of trust, collegiality and support. It's easy to add a line at the end of your correspondence with a simple offer to help (try something like: 'Please don't hesitate to let me know if there is anything else I can assist you with,' or 'Please let me know if you have any questions'). Something that seems quick and formulaic for you can make a real difference to the recipient.

Anticipate questions (and suggest answers)

Particularly in the context of internal correspondence, try not to turn up with only questions. It's fine to have questions – that's what your supervisors are there for, after all – but make sure that you've also had a reasonable go at providing the answer (i.e. make sure your role is active and not passive). In your written correspondence, aim to include a short summary of the question, followed by a brief statement of what you think the answer might be (and the basis for your conclusion), plus any steps you took to solve the problem on your own. It doesn't matter too much if you're miles off. The point is that you're actively advancing your own development – it shows that you care, you tried, and you're eager to learn.

A NOTE ON READING EMAILS

The flood of emails that enter your new inbox upon starting out as a legal professional can make the 'delete all' button seem like an irresistible temptation. But be warned: a habit of allowing emails to go unread can have big consequences in the long term. Missed correspondence, questions or instructions can result in serious communication issues.

Best practice is to trawl through all emails, open all and review all – even just to check that they're not relevant to you. Only then should you delight in the delete button.

Email etiquette

If you're entering a professional industry, there's a good chance that much of your working life will be eaten away by email (sorry about that). As a result, it's essential to master the basics of conducting an email exchange in a business context. The following guidelines will give you some idea of where to start:

Format

- Make sure text is generously set out, with paragraphs broken down to represent different topics, and enough space between each point for your reader to follow your thoughts.
- Use a double space at the end of each sentence to make the text clear.
- Make use of sub-headings, bullet points, lists, etc. – these can all become essential tools in the crafting of an artful, effective email.

Structure

- Place your main point first, with analysis and supporting evidence/data following in the body of the email.
- If you need a recipient to take action, highlight this clearly (for example, by including a note to them by name, underlined or bold to make it stand out).
- If you're proposing action/next steps that you intend to take, make sure they are clearly set out. The same applies for any permissions/sign-off you need from the recipient of your email.

Purpose

- The intent and purpose of your email should be clear from the first few lines. Is your email useful? What is it intended to achieve? What action needs to happen next?
- Do you know the recipient? If not, can you find out a little about them in order to be aware of their involvement in your matter, and the level of legal understanding they might (or might not) have?
- After asking yourself the questions above, restructure the text to make the intent and purpose obvious to the recipient. There are enough meandering, vague emails in the life of any business professional – make sure yours isn't one of them.

Responses

- It might seem exhausting to respond to every direct email as quickly as possible. However, in return for your efforts, you'll be rewarded with a degree of flexibility and trust – if the sender knows that you've read their email and you're working on dealing with their issue, you're free to structure your own time in a more flexible way. Even sending a quick holding response (you've seen their email; you're dealing with it) can do the job.

Content

- Are you confident about every point you've made in your email? If you're stating factual information, have you verified it? Do you understand each individual line of text you're writing? It might sound obvious, but it's easy to paraphrase something you've heard from a supervisor without fully understanding it. Take the time to work it out. On a purely practical level, you might end up with a call from the recipient, asking you to explain the correspondence (and you don't want to have to reveal that you don't actually understand your own message).
- It's fine not to include a definitive conclusion. Perhaps the law is unclear in a particular area, or there are no relevant precedents. When dealing with ambiguity, it's acceptable to say that you don't have a clear answer – just make sure you know *why* you've reached that position, and outline the steps you took to get there (as well as any extra information you need). You can also set out the different scenarios you considered, if appropriate.
- Does the content need to be checked with a supervising lawyer before sending it out? It's best practice to double check for all emails (even the prosaic ones!) until you get a sense of what is good to go out without review.

- Are you including specific references (such as case law, regulations or statutes)? Have you double-checked for accuracy, and to make sure they're all fully up to date?

> **A NOTE ON HITTING 'SEND'**
>
> Does your subject line relate to the content of the email? Do you have the right people in the addressee/'(b)cc' line? Have you checked the whole email chain to make sure it's appropriate for all recipients to review? Have you attached the correct documents? Are all names spelled correctly?
>
> This might seem obvious, but when you're experiencing your first few months of business emails, you're in prime habit-building stage. Setting your foundations well means you can develop great business practices for the rest of your career.
>
> For a more detailed checklist, see **Checklist 1.1** at the end of this chapter.

Client communication

Law firms are service providers, delivering an end-product to a paying client. As a new joiner in the workplace, there may be some occasions where you are expected to be the point of contact for such a client. In these situations, you need to exercise particular care and caution in your written communications.

For your first couple of months, always check if your supervisor or another senior team member can cast an eye over your work before it goes out. If it's not possible in the moment, stick to making statements that you know to be true, and avoid over-ambitious deadline or work product promises.

In terms of tone, it's best to mirror the voice of the client, as set out in their own correspondence (although, of course, never if the client sets an inappropriate precedent). If in doubt, stay on the side of over-formality. Stop communication when things get out of your depth, and always aim to have a senior member of your own team copied into the correspondence (or at least fully updated with the status of the conversation).

The art of note-taking

Why to do it

As a junior lawyer, one easy way to add value is to be the designated 'note-taker' of the group at meetings or during calls. A proofread, typed-up set of notes will be a much-appreciated gift to your senior colleagues, and the process of recording and reviewing notes will greatly advance your own understanding.

It may also be the case that points of nuance are lost in conversation or misunderstood between team members. If you are taking contemporaneous notes, you can position yourself as the figure of authority to whom others will turn to 'check the record'. Turning up with notebook or laptop prepared will also make you look one step ahead of the game.

How to do it

When thinking about how to take notes, be sensitive to your surroundings. If your colleagues are typing away, follow suit. If everyone else in a meeting is making handwritten comments, do the same. Avoid drawing attention to yourself with loudly tapping laptop keys in the midst of a quiet meeting.

If you use shorthand, make sure your notes are readable and presentable. Don't record anything that you wouldn't be willing to share with others – you never know where a written record will end up. If you're in a meeting or call with multiple participants, consider preparing your first draft in the form of a script, clearly identifying who said what. That way, if a point needs to be clarified further down the line, you have a record not only of what was said, but by whom.

One final point: make sure your filing system is considered, intentional and workable. Junior lawyers are often a repository for information – supervisors may call on you to produce a document, email or attachment with urgency. Be ready to step in and add value: know your email folders inside out, and – if you retain paper copies of documents – make sure your filing standards are set high (and that they don't slip a few weeks into the job!).

A NOTE ON CONFIDENTIALITY

Exercise caution in enthusiastic note-taking during situations that may call for some degree of sensitivity (for example, confidential client meetings or calls). In these kinds of situations, it's best to double check with someone senior.

Mistakes destroy credibility

It's an irritating truth – but a truth nonetheless – that simple errors in written communication can instantly take a writer's credibility to zero. Think about correspondence you receive from 'authority' voices, such as your bank or your doctor. You'd probably be suspicious if the writing contained obvious mistakes or typos. The same applies for your business writing. You want the reader to trust you – not only for the purposes of enhancing your own reputation, but also to make sure that your communication moves the project forwards.

You should always proofread (see below), but also use back-ups such as a simple spell-check or forming the habit of reading your draft out loud before sending. For more serious pieces of writing, see if a colleague can take a quick look before you circulate. It's often easy for others to spot our mistakes, and annoyingly difficult to spot our own.

Why bother to proofread?

Working on the basis that mistakes destroy credibility, it's safe to say that proofreading will become a crucial tool in your skillset. Not only is it likely to help you avoid obvious errors, but you'll also get a better sense of the structure and format of the overall piece.

A few tips for the proofreading professional:

- Scan once for mistakes in spelling, grammar and formatting. Scan a second time to review the content – it's difficult to do both at the same time.
- When proofreading your content, make sure you have a coherent structure and flow to the writing. Is your main point obvious within the first couple of lines of text? Can the recipient easily figure out what it means and what to do next?
- You may need to step away from the draft for a few hours to get an enhanced perspective – it's easy to overlook to obvious mistakes when you've been immersed in the same piece of work for hours.
- If you know a colleague has been working on a piece of writing for some time, offering to proofread (if they would find it helpful) can earn office credit. Importantly, it also means they might do the same for you in return.

A NOTE ON WHEN TO PROOFREAD

Don't confine your proofreading routine to the bigger, more involved pieces of work. Get into the habit of proofreading every piece of written work that you send out – a quick email, an internal note, thoughts from meetings, etc. Building this habit will set you up well in the future, and you'll begin to develop a reputation as someone who writes with precision and accuracy.

Good grammar

While it's true that grammar is fluid and varied, it's also true that writing in non-standard English will cause your recipient to question your abilities – so best to stick to the formalities used by everyone around you. If you're unsure, or if a sentence doesn't quite sound right, double check the grammar online, or run it past a colleague. Reading your own work out loud often gives a helpful indication of whether or not your grammar is accurate.

A NOTE ON THE RULES

It may seem tempting to go with what 'feels' right in terms of grammar, but learning the underlying rules can actually be a shortcut to getting it right in the long term. You may even find that navigating grammatical predicaments in the future isn't so difficult after all …

There are a couple of great resources online. Try, for example:

- Oxford Dictionaries (**www.oxforddictionaries.com**)
- Grammarly (**wwwgrammarly.com**)

Legal references

At some point, you're likely to be given a piece of research that involves a deep dive into a piece of legislation or case law. It's essential, of course, to fully understand the legal background, and to be able to support your conclusions with legal authority. However, when presenting your findings, make sure you draft for your intended recipient. For example, if you're writing an explanatory note for a client, be mindful of your use of technical legal language – it's likely that the client will have little to no understanding of your references. In these circumstances, it might be helpful to simplify your drafting, remove excessive legal language (after checking and confirming your conclusions with your supervisor), and double check that you haven't made any assumptions about the knowledge of the reader.

If you are asked to draft some research findings for a more senior lawyer, it's fine – and helpful – to include legal references. Make sure, however, that your drafting remains reader-friendly. For example, can you make each case reference stand out by using italics, or bold font? Can you hyperlink any relevant resources within the body of the email, or attach case summaries where relevant? Can you condense your understanding of the case law or legislation into a couple of carefully drafted sentences?

Regardless of your intended recipient, it's helpful to test the draft for readability. Try to proofread as if you had no knowledge of the topic or subject, and make changes to aid understanding where necessary.

A NOTE ON THE DETAILS

The details matter. From the way you address your correspondence to the consistency of tone and style; from the precision of your language to the impact your message has on the recipient – these details matter. Think of the individual details as the foundation of your correspondence, and pay them close attention.

Carefully worded, well-considered written work sets the stage for a relationship of trust, professionalism and clarity. And, of course, how you do the small things is often a reflection of how you do everything else.

Technical terminology

Many areas of practice are overflowing with their own technical terminology (in other words, 'jargon'). If you're in one of these practice areas, it's worth keeping a personal record of 'defined terms'. Every time you hear a new piece of jargon, write it down, and dedicate some time to look up the definition online. Keep your personal dictionary to hand: the more you use it, the more helpful it will be.

Developing this habit may seem time-consuming at first, but it will put you in the uncommon position of actually knowing what people are talking about when they use technical terms. You'd be surprised at how many people quietly navigate themselves through a jargon-heavy industry without really understanding what the jargon means. Remember: it may even be the case that the person casually using the term doesn't truly understand its meaning or relevance.

If you're in a context that allows for it, ask the person using the jargon if they can explain what it means. In any event, asking genuine, thoughtful questions will always give the impression of intelligent curiosity. Jargon can be used to obscure a point that its user is unsure about – it's your right to call it out (politely). In fact, this is a helpful test to apply to your own use of jargon – if you use a technical term, would you be able to explain it, with precision, if you were asked for its definition? If not, best to stick to language you know and fully understand.

Precedents and standard forms

As lawyers, precedents and standard forms can often be a great aid to kick-start the drafting process. Precedents enable you to use a document that's already been peer-reviewed and proven to work effectively; standard forms make sure you capture all the relevant information and meet specific legal criteria. However, both should be used with caution, and neither should be regarded as a shortcut. It may (and often will) be the case that your individual scenario differs from the precedent in a number of ways. As a junior lawyer, it's your role to identify the differences and make sure that you adapt the precedent accordingly.

As you work with your precedent or standard form document, ask yourself the following questions:

- What specific set of circumstances does this template document deal with?
- How does my current scenario differ from this?
- What kind of drafting is needed to deal with the changes?
- Are there any new legal requirements, practices or guidelines that might come into play for my current scenario, that would not have been relevant for the template document?
- If my current document ends up with significant departures from the precedent, do I need to make a note to warn against using my document as a precedent in the future?

In general, make sure that the lawyer reviewing your work is aware that you've used the precedent or standard form (it's helpful to attach it, along with your own work, when you send it to them for review). You can add a brief explanation about why you thought the precedent was helpful, and the ways you checked to ensure that it was tailored to your individual set of circumstances.

Receiving comments

So, you've perfected your piece of written work and you're ready to hand it over for review. It's easy to think that you can sit back and wait for comments – but, for those wanting to get one step ahead, consider the following questions:

- In what kind of format would the reviewing lawyer like to receive the work? The reviewer may prefer an email attachment, or printed copy; they may want it single- or double-sided, or stapled, clipped or tabbed. They may want to review alongside associated documents, or against a precedent. They may want a document containing your internal notes, or a 'clean' version prepared for external circulation.

  The best way to navigate the diversity of requests from various supervisors is to actually *ask* them, and then make a note of the way in which they prefer to review. With a record of what they like (or don't like) when it comes to reviewing your work, you'll be well-placed to tailor your finished work product to their requests in future.

- Have you considered what it would be like to receive the work for review?
  - Have you given the reviewer enough time to meet external deadlines?
  - Have you given them enough context to your work, so that they share in your background knowledge?
  - Have you made sure to double check any uncertainties or outstanding questions before turning in your work?

Considering your work from a reviewer's perspective can be a valuable process: it's often not until we put ourselves in the shoes of another lawyer that we can see what might need to change. Think about anything that would make the process of review easier from the perspective of the supervising lawyer (or, if you can, ask them directly).

Incorporating comments

Once you've received comments on your work, set aside some time to work through them. Figuring out your own system for capturing and incorporating each comment can be helpful: consider numbering or crossing off each marked change as you work through the document. Where you don't understand a change, make a note to follow up. Be careful of assuming that supervising lawyers are correct every time: it's your job to make sure that you pick up on any misunderstandings or errors in the mark-up, as well as producing a revised draft.

In general – and this applies to all work you do as a junior lawyer – avoid incorporating changes to documents that you don't fully understand. There may be occasions, in a time-pressured scenario, where you can double-check the change with the supervising lawyer, and (once you have their sign-off), mark any areas of confusion for a later debrief. The aim, however, should be to understand changes as you make them, and never blindly incorporate comments – even from a more senior lawyer – where you don't understand the context.

Comparisons and redlines

Receiving comparison documents (and 'redline' documents, where two documents are compared using electronic software) is a common feature of trainee life. Be aware, however, that documents showing comparison changes can be altered to show up only certain changes or amendments. If you have your own redline software, it can be helpful to double check redlines received from external parties against your own versions.

A NOTE ON SETTING THE BAR

As you start your training contract, consider where you'll be setting the bar for yourself. What will your minimum standards look like?

- Aim, for example, to always have your work free of obvious errors (a system of drafting, proofreading and redrafting will help).
- Make sure that you've kept closely to the instructions you were given, and you haven't deviated too far off track without running your intentions past your supervisor.
- Keep to deadlines and time-limits – or rearrange them (with plenty of notice) to make them more realistic.
- When drafting substantive correspondence, it might be helpful (if time allows) to leave your message in a draft folder for a few hours, and return to it with fresh eyes.
- Internal notes and cover emails are helpful for explaining your thought processes.
- If you get stuck or confused about certain points, make sure that you explain the issue to your supervisor, and describe any steps you took to solve it (additional research, looking at other resources, asking other team members, etc.).

Setting some basic guidelines for your own work product will help you uphold high standards for yourself, even in the midst of a busy working week.

Common mistakes

The mistake: hiding a lack of knowledge in complexity

If your written work starts to take the form of an academic treatise, try this: ask yourself whether you could easily explain the point to a child. A lack of understanding is easily masked in long, convoluted explanations or an overuse of jargon. Challenge yourself to simplify, and identify content that can easily be deleted. Take another look at the statements you're left with. If you were challenged on each point, could you provide a brief, comprehensive explanation?

The mistake: spending too long on a task, or not spending long enough

As a junior lawyer, you're often caught between opposing impulses: you want to get the work out as quickly as possible (especially if there's an urgent matter or deal that depends on it), but you also want it to be your best possible work (especially if it's for external circulation).

One good tip is to ask the supervising lawyer how long the work is expected to take. Receiving an honest answer will help you to plan and structure your time – and the answer is likely to be based on experience, giving you a useful 'real-life' starting point for mapping out your next steps. This also has the benefit of making the supervising lawyer actively consider the work from your perspective, perhaps providing you with a more realistic sense of timing.

Remember that you always have two aspects to balance here: the need for you to be efficient with your time, and the need for you to expand your own learning and development. Finding the appropriate balance between the two tensions will be your responsibility every time you're assigned a task.

The mistake: writing as if your recipient shares your understanding

In general, it's helpful to assume that the recipient doesn't have the background knowledge you have. If your work is intended for external circulation, this rule is especially helpful – often, your client won't have the benefit of the legal background or framework that you can take for granted when communicating with other lawyers.

Even on an internal level, however, there's something to be said for writing from first principles. Setting out your conclusions in a way that shows where you started, how you progressed the reasoning and where you ended up is often much more helpful than jumping in and assuming that the recipient is on the same page. You also never really know where your work might end up, so you should generally draft as if external circulation could happen.

Construct your work as you would a maths problem – have you set out the reasoning so that someone could go back and check each step? Have you documented each point, and made sure that the conclusion follows in a logical chain from the premises? Setting your thought process out clearly and with obvious, rational progression, will facilitate the work of the reviewer (and will no doubt help to clarify your own thoughts in the process). You can always use footnotes for additional explanation, if you don't want to over-complicate the text.

The mistake: saying something pointless

Ever remember being told that if you don't have anything good to say, don't say anything at all? The same applies here: either make a point (and make it effectively and well), or wait until you've gathered enough information to properly contribute to a discussion or hand in a decent piece of written work.

Options for taking further action when you don't feel like you have enough to say (yet) include the following:

- asking for feedback on an interim draft;

- compiling a structure/summary, and submitting it as a 'work in progress';
- putting together a set of questions which will provide you with the information you need to move forwards, and finding the appropriate person to ask; and/or
- using a precedent (with care) – on which, see more above.

The point is not about being perfect – you should expect to make mistakes, and not feel bad about them (after all, the fastest way to learn is usually through real-life experience). Instead, it's about *not* being the person who sends hastily drafted or incomplete work, or the person who generates correspondence simply for the sake of sending something out. Make sure all of your written work has a clear, defined purpose, and you'll find that people are more receptive to receiving it.

The mistake: failing to format, structure and craft your correspondence

As a trainee, you'll find that you can earn yourself a lot of credit by making sure your correspondence is flawless in appearance. It might seem basic and even frustrating (after all those years of hard academic study at university), but the truth is that a perfectly formatted document can go a long way towards enhancing a reputation of competence and reliability. Poorly structured work – however insightful or impressive in substance – looks lazy (at best) and incompetent (at worst).

With that in mind, put some effort into structuring, crafting and preparing your piece of work. Is it easy to read? Have you used features such as bullet points, numbered lists or other reader-friendly formatting? Is it crafted with your conclusion first, and your supporting evidence following later? Does it clearly set out the question that was asked, and any assumptions you had to make?

Reading and responding to emails on the go (i.e. on your phone) can often encourage informality. See if you can set aside time to properly read and respond to messages, even if you're away from your desk. In this context, a little attention to detail will go a long way (and don't ever underestimate the dangers that come with a careless use of autocorrect …).

One final point. Avoid assuming that your writing style will miraculously develop on its own. It's worth putting some effort into developing your tone and voice. Look at the correspondence of those you work with. Is there anything you admire? How can you integrate elements of their style into your own work? Ask for feedback if you're not getting it. Keep yourself accountable: review your own email correspondence and ask yourself – is this the best I can create?

Finally, before hitting send, run through the following checklist to pick up any lingering errors.

CHECKLIST 1.1: CLIENT-READY COMMUNICATION

1. Is my email addressed to the correct recipients? Checking – and double-checking – the recipient list on all email correspondence is essential. Accidentally copying the wrong person on confidential material could be a breach of compliance policies. One way to protect against a dramatic email failure is to add the names of the recipients as the final step, so you can take a second to double check them.
2. Have I copied (and/or bcc'ed) the correct people?
3. Is the title of the email clear and error-free? Does it relate directly to the subject matter of the email? Note that long chains of email correspondence can often switch topic without the subject-line of the email reflecting the change. Double check to see if it would be helpful to update the title in line with evolving discussions.
4. Are all names spelled correctly? Have I opened and closed the email with appropriate greetings/formalities? If this is my first email in a chain of correspondence, have I introduced myself with sufficient clarity?
5. Have I attached the correct attachments? Have I mentioned an attachment in the body of the email, but forgotten to attach it? Is the attachment labelled clearly, with the correct date, and free of internal drafting notes? Is the attachment in a form easily accessible for any recipient? Does the attachment need to be sent securely? Remember that large files may be rejected by some email servers. When sending through large attachments, it's best to send a follow-up email – without attachments – to confirm that the recipient has received everything.
6. Where I cross-refer to documents, have I made the recipient's job as easy as possible (for example, by accurately describing or summarising particular provisions, or by hyperlinking relevant resources)?
7. Is the tone of my email appropriate and consistent?
8. Is my email clearly arranged, with a readable, logical structure?
9. If there are next steps to be taken in this matter, have I clearly set them out? Do all recipients know what is expected from them (if anything) going forwards?

Chapter 2

Communication: the spoken word

Having something to say, and knowing how to say it

This chapter is about the spoken word: how to get yourself heard, how to make sure you're remembered, and – perhaps most importantly – how to listen effectively to the voices of others. The following pages will lead you through the terrifying topic of office presentations, via the (equally terrifying) world of meetings, pitches and conference calls. Master the basics, and you'll be on your way to delivering and receiving a spoken message with ease and excellence.

Crafting a presentation

Whether it's an informal discussion with your supervisor, or preparation for a client pitch, the following checklist will help you map out what you want to say and how you want to say it.

CHECKLIST 2.1: PREPARING PRESENTATIONS

1. **What are you trying to say?** Start by getting clear on the heart of the presentation. What are you trying to communicate to your audience? What is the core concept that you want your audience to absorb? Perhaps you're opening up a discussion on a new or contentious piece of law; perhaps you're trying to convince or persuade your audience to adopt a particular viewpoint. Whatever it is, make sure you know it, and work to make each subtopic – even down to each individual slide of your presentation – directly relevant to the point.
2. **How long have you got?** It's fine to over-prepare material, but be prepared to cut down in the event you run out of time. A good approach is to go through your notes, flagging specific sections that could be jettisoned without losing the substance of the presentation. If you're finding this difficult, it might be that you have overcomplicated things.

   You may also find it helpful to have markers in your notes to indicate timing – for example, a note in the margins at the point where you should be halfway through. As well as taking the pressure off (you don't have to keep watch-checking throughout), it ensures you don't realise the time is up as you're just finishing your introduction.

   Also, ensure you actually have a watch (unless you know the room has a reliable, visible clock). Nothing worse than a speaker periodically glancing down at their phone.

3. **What's the story?** Humans are driven by narrative – we're hard-wired to latch on to a gripping story. Capitalise on this with the following tricks:

   - On a macro level, think about the story of the presentation as a whole. As you structure the script, plan the journey for the audience: give the background, show the eventual destination and then elaborate on the pathway to get them there. At the end, recap (tell them what you've just told them).
   - On a micro-level, think about individual stories you can tell throughout the presentation. Can you open with a story that sets the scene? Can you give a personal testimony, or an individual narrative that illustrates your points?
   - Think about ways you can have the audience reflecting on their own stories. This could be done by posing questions ('How has this issue affected your work?'), or leaving time for reflections and note-taking ('Take a couple of minutes to reflect on a time in your life when you experienced this issue'). It's one thing to get the audience to sit still and consume your information. It's another thing entirely to get them to *feel* something.

4. **Notes, slides, and safety nets.** Think about what you'll be taking with you when you stand up to present. Slides are great – and there's research to back up the claim that some people are natural 'visual learners' – but make sure you're not using them for the wrong reasons. These include: fear of eye contact with your audience, lack of preparation, and an inability to cut down content into an easily explained message.

   Ask yourself: would I be able to give this talk in the event of a catastrophic IT-related failure? If you could, then slides may be a great way to supplement your talk – just make sure they stay concise (two or three lines per slide is usually enough) and don't distract the audience (avoid strange graphics, sounds and jargon).

   If you're braving it without slides and just taking a set of speaker notes, keep them concise – preferably in shorthand – so you can spend maximum time engaging with the audience. Making frequent eye contact will help you read the room (are they bored, distracted or looking at their phones?) and respond accordingly.
5. **Are you stage-ready?** Running through your presentation is essential preparation – a full dress rehearsal isn't necessary, but talking it through to yourself will help you to plan the pace. If you have time, film or record yourself going through the content, and play it back (yes, it's painful to watch, but it's also incredibly valuable).

   Can you pick up on your areas of weakness? Can you spot moments where you display discomfort, or show an uncertainty with the subject matter? Make notes; hold yourself accountable. Give yourself feedback as you would do for a friend (or see if a friend will watch your recording and give their honest opinion).

A NOTE ON HOLDING SPACE:

Running a meeting, presenting to groups or explaining your thoughts to your supervisor: all of these activities require cultivated attention to the other people in the room. The idea of 'holding space' for other people is different to just organising the logistics of an event: it requires full presence and attention. It requires you to be focused, alert and receptive. It requires you to not be thinking about your plans for the weekend, or having a quick check of social media under the desk.

It's a simple concept but very rarely put into practice, especially in a work environment. Practising being present with others – 'holding space', rather than just being in physical attendance – can be immensely powerful, and will easily set you apart from others.

Speaking for an audience

There's a difference between speaking up at a weekly team meeting and speaking for an 'audience'. At some point, your task morphs from something you don't think twice about into something that fills you with dread (or, at the very least, nervous anticipation). Here are a handful of tips to use when faced with the opportunity to speak to a large audience:

- **Stand up.** The 'power pose' has gathered a lot of public discussion, and for good reason – standing in a pose that exudes confidence and strength can often make you feel more competent. Walk into the room with self-assurance, lengthen your spine and take up some space: even if you feel like you're just pretending to be confident, it's likely that no one will know the difference.
- **Make eye contact and smile.** There's nothing worse than being an audience member for a speaker who looks like they're about to pass out from nerves. By meeting the eyes of your audience and smiling reassuringly, you'll put everyone at ease – including yourself. Remember that the audience are on your side: believe it or not, they want you to succeed!
- **Project yourself.** Speak a little louder and slower than you normally would. Even if it feels uncomfortable, you're more likely to be criticised for being too quiet than too loud (however, if you've got a microphone, obviously avoid shouting into it).
- **Have a get-out ready.** Good back-ups to use in the event of an awkward silence are:
  - asking the audience if they have any questions;
  - summarising what you've been saying;
  - telling the audience an anecdote (keep it related to the topic of the presentation);

  - getting your audience to turn to the person next to them and discuss a point you've just covered; and/or
  - sipping – slowly! – from a glass of water.

  In general, though, don't be too afraid of silence. Think of it less as an absence of content and more as the *presence* of an effective presentation tool. Pauses, breaks and moments of reflection can be incredibly persuasive, and show the audience that you have it all under control. Remember that those agonisingly silent moments will be passing much more slowly in your own head than they will be for everyone else in the room.
- **Get moving.** Instead of getting stuck behind a table or podium, see if you can work the stage: walk the space, speak to the entirety of the audience, get comfortable with natural hand gestures. Practise in the privacy of your own room until you get the hang of it. On the day, get to the presentation location early and spend some time familiarising yourself with the landscape.

A NOTE ON READING A ROOM

As people start to fill up the space of your presentation room, take a quick scan of the audience. Are people sitting in groups, or in departmental teams, or scattering throughout the room? Can you sense the audience's level of energy? Are most people settling, or are audience members still checking email, or chatting to their neighbours? If it's a lunchtime presentation, be aware that people may be bringing in food (and probably making it their primary focus for the first part of the session). Tailor your content to the context – delay any elements of audience participation until you have their full attention.

With smaller groups, there may be an opportunity to check in with the group personally. Ask them how they are and how they're feeling – listen carefully, and shape your presentation accordingly. Watch out for subtle cues (body language, facial expressions) and begin to build a picture of the overall group dynamic.

Armed with the information from your observations, you can start to make a couple of guesses about how your audience will respond to you and your work. Knowing your subject matter well enough to be able to deliver the presentation that the audience want to receive (rather than the one you want to give them) will make all the difference.

Holding meetings

Organising and facilitating meetings is a task that's likely to land on your desk frequently as a junior lawyer. The following checklist will make sure you don't forget the basics.

CHECKLIST 2.2: MEETING PREPARATION

1. **Sort the logistics.** If you're responsible for organising the meeting, make sure you've covered off the basic logistical elements. Do you have a room? Is it booked for the right amount of time? Have you sent all attendees an appropriate invitation? Have you organised office passes for external guests, or let the reception desk know they'll be arriving? Do you need refreshments, or any IT aids set up? Are there enough chairs?

   As with any presentation context, it's a good idea to be the first one in the room – well prepared, and ready to go – especially if the meeting is hosted in your name.
2. **Pack the essentials.** For meetings with people you haven't yet met, remember to take your business card. You can (tactfully) hand these out as people take their seats – it's a good way of ensuring that people can put a name to a face. If others present you with their own business cards, make a mental note of their name (a good trick is to say their name again in your own greeting to them, after they introduce themselves).

   Make sure you have something on which to take notes – either a laptop or notebook. Read the room – if everyone has laptops, go ahead and set up; if everyone is taking notes by hand, follow their lead. Remember not to use a notebook that contains visible notes from other client matters. Making notes on spare sheets of paper can also sometimes come across as a little careless.
3. **Kick off with control.** If you're running the meeting, establish authority by producing and circulating an agenda ahead of the appointment. When you have everyone in the room, you can kick off by introducing yourself, thanking everyone for attending, and re-reading your agenda aloud. Is the group agreed on the ultimate outcome you're working towards? From here it's an easy segue into the first agenda item, after checking that no one has any questions.

   Keep everyone on track by watching the clock, and make sure you leave enough time to get through all the items on your list. If the discussion slides off-course, you can – politely! – interject to steer everyone back (try something along the lines of: 'Just bearing in mind the limited time, I'd suggest we stick to the specific question at hand, and reserve other points for later discussion').
4. **Finish well.** At the end, make sure people have an opportunity to ask questions. Remember: if it's possible to wrap up early and still cover everything, it enables people to get a slice of time back that they thought was lost (which can result in a great recollection of the meeting from their perspective).
5. **Follow up.** The first thing you do post-meeting should be to collect and review your notes. It's easy to feel like you need to dive straight in and start on tasks that came out of the discussion, but collecting your thoughts first will give you a valuable foundation for any work that comes next. This also gives you an opportunity to clarify any uncertainties while the other participants still have a clear recollection of what happened. Was the overall outcome of the meeting achieved? If not, why not, and what can be done about it?

   If appropriate – usually most relevant for internal purposes – you can send an edited version of your meeting notes around to the team (and even if you don't send them, make sure they're filed somewhere in your office or inbox).

When following up with external clients, a short email summary of the event might be useful – check with your supervisor before sending this out. At the very least, any follow-up communication must ensure that each attendee is clear on their next steps. Ask yourself: would the recipient of this follow-up message know – preferably within the first couple of lines – exactly what action they need to take next? If not, redraft until there's no room for doubt, missed messages or misunderstandings.

Finally, if there's an appropriate opportunity to receive feedback on your own performance, don't forget to ask for it.

Communication styles

As you make your first steps into the world of work, you'll quickly learn one thing: everyone has a different way of communicating. You'll find people with whom you seem to click within a moment, and others who – quite frankly – could be speaking another language, for all the mixed messages and missed signals going on between the two of you. Relax – diversity of communication is a feature of almost every workplace (and can make for a richness of culture and creativity). To make things simple, here are some pointers on the communication styles you're likely to encounter in the office:

Driver

This is the kind of person that makes decisions (and lets you know about them). Drivers are ambitious, motivated and often vocal about their ideas. They're great to have on a project that needs pushing forward, but not so great when it comes to hearing out quieter team members, or engaging in reflective analysis.

How to handle: the first step is to make sure your 'driver' knows they've been heard. An acknowledgment – in person or by email – of their ideas is likely to go a long way. You can facilitate this by demonstrating that they've made a contribution – openly thanking them for their input, or circulating revised drafts showing their comments – and always keep them fully updated on progress.

Influencer

Influencers like to be in control – just like drivers – but the method is somewhat subtler. Influencers may have a job title to go with their power, or they may not. Your office influencer may be the managing partner, a long-standing secretary, or the junior associate who organises the office social events. Either way, you want to make sure you have your influencers on-side: they'll be invaluable when it comes to steering projects, initiatives and opportunities in your favour.

How to handle: if you have a new idea you're pushing forwards, get your influencer on-side by taking the time to explain the concept and seek their feedback. Influencers are powerful for a reason – their opinion matters. Integrate your influencer's thoughts, get them to promote you to their circle, and harness the psychology of the crowd by associating yourself with their leader.

Grounded

Grounded colleagues are likely to be good communicators – in general, they'll be consistent, dependable and competent. On the flip side, they're less likely to be innovative, overly creative or too ambitious (they often make great lawyers – their risk aversion and reliability are highly sought-after traits).

How to handle: make sure your grounded colleague stays well up to date with the status of any matter or project: they should be fully in the loop with your next steps long before you take them. Avoid unnerving your grounded colleague with unexpected initiatives – keep communication channels open, simple and frequently utilised.

Conscientious

Your conscientious colleagues are the ones who'll double check your work – and then return to take a third look at it. They're the ones who email you late at night with something they've just remembered (and which is no doubt keeping them up with its importance). Your conscientious colleagues – much like their grounded counterparts – make great lawyers, but these perfectionist tendencies can also slow down progress (especially during busy periods in the office).

How to handle: as with the grounded lawyer, make sure your conscientious colleagues are fully updated – however, in this case, factor in ample time for comments, questions and observations. If you need their thoughts on something, it's helpful to remind them of any deadlines. From your perspective, be prepared to incorporate those last-minute details to help your conscientious colleague sleep a little easier.

Starting and ending well

Let's be honest, the average office presentation often follows the same old format. Speaker stands up, introduces self and topic, launches into the content, and wraps up with a summary, followed by a brief question and answer session. But you're not just trying to deliver an average office presentation. You want something that makes people look up from their iPhones; something that makes them forget about their cafeteria sandwich for a few minutes. You want to be remembered.

So, how to do it? Research has indicated that recollections of an event focus on the 'peak' (i.e. the most intense moment) and the end of the experience. If you're delivering a presentation on a fairly dry topic, it's worth bearing in mind that people tend to remember moments of light relief with greater clarity, as it stands out as a contrast to the rest of your material.

Starting well and ending well are therefore essential. Here are a few pointers to help you map out your performance:

- **Small group presentations.** Kick off by getting everyone to give their own introductions (their name, and perhaps something about their background or expertise).
- **Storytelling.** Everyone loves a narrative.
- **Questions.** Ask a question. Get the audience on the edge of their seats by calling on someone to answer. Seek their opinion; get their experience; engage with them.
- **Props.** Is there anything relevant to your presentation that you can use to visibly demonstrate a point? Think creatively: if you're talking about property law, could you use physical maps and models? If you're discussing capital markets developments, could you bring in a paper copy of the financial press, and read out extracts to support your points? It often doesn't matter what the actual 'prop' is: it's about grabbing the audience's attention.
- **Quotes.** Use sparingly, but to great effect. Quoting some kind of inspirational figure can be a good opener or closer (perhaps even try referring back to an opening quote at the close of the presentation).
- **Scenarios.** Set up a hypothetical scenario to frame your problem. You can open this with the phrase: 'Imagine the scene …'. Bonus points if you use audience member names as your 'characters', or call on individual attendees to suggest what might happen next, or how the situation might be resolved.

Handouts and takeaways

It can be useful for your audience to have a short handout (it enables them to physically take your presentation with them as they walk back into their week). But be careful that the handout doesn't remove the magic from your spoken words – you want the focus (and the suspense) to be on what you're saying, so avoid distributing your conclusions in advance. Handouts should be brief, and preferably illustrate only a couple of key points, or outline only the general structure. They should also include some space in which audience members can take notes.

How to be remembered

In the office context, it's not easy for people to remember a brief presentation – after all, you've heard hundreds of them before. Their minds will be on their next email, or on their next meeting (or on what time they can head home for the day). How can you make sure you live on in the minds of your audience? Try the following:

- Summarise your content at the end of your talk. Use the power of recap to initiate reflection in your audience.
- End in an unexpected way. Can you leave the audience wanting more by ending on an open question, or on a reflection about the future?
- Let them take away a physical object. Think about what you could leave the audience with – for example, a short summary handout, or a card containing a quote or key message (and, for external presentations, your contact details).
- Send a follow-up email. Get back to the top of people's minds (and inboxes) by sending an email out in the few hours after the talk. Thank the audience for coming, recap on what happened, and give them a few resources for further reading or research.
- Ask people for their feedback. If you know any audience members, drop them a call – or visit – after your presentation. Ask for honest feedback (and take notes!). Seek to incorporate the feedback into your next presentation. If you don't know the audience personally, you can welcome general feedback at the end of your presentation: provide your email address, and let people know they can approach you with questions or comments.

Speak, then listen, then speak

By now, you've perfected your presentation and mastered your speaking skills, but this is only half of the story. To get ahead as a speaker, you'll also need to learn how to listen.

Why refine your listening skills?

Done well, active listening will become one of the most powerful tools in your portfolio. Listening enables you to more accurately understand the other person – this, in turn, enables you to deliver value to them in a uniquely specialised way. Not only will this process forge stronger connections and career relationships, but it will also give you great power. By combining others' thoughts and opinions with your own, you'll be able to craft work that genuinely adds value and exceeds expectations. Convinced? Read on for the step-by-step guide to mastering the skill.

How to practise active listening

- Lean in – using your body language (on which, more later – see **Chapter 3**), signal to the other person that you're engaged and interested. Position yourself in an open way (i.e. without your arms folded) towards the speaker. When they say something significant, or if they change their tone, a subtle lean towards them can be effective.
- Get ready – if you can tell someone is working to elicit a certain emotion (humour, shock or curiosity), get ready with an appropriate reaction. Showing that you understand where the speaker is going (whether it be through a smile, nod or other non-verbal cue) will give them confidence that you're on the journey with them.
- The recap – at the end of an explanation, a great tactic is to recap what the speaker has been saying. Try: 'So, what I understand from what you've been saying is …' Perhaps finish your explanation with this question: 'Is my understanding correct?' This gives your speaker an opportunity to jump in and let you know if you've missed anything obvious, and builds rapport between speaker and listener.

On the other side: being the audience

By now, you'll be well equipped to have an audience engaged, entranced and enchanted – but what about the reverse situation? How can you use *someone else's* presentation to enhance your own professional development? Consider the following:

1. The golden rule: always have a question

A quick, reliable way to make sure you're a fully present audience member is to ask yourself: what question would I ask if I were called upon? It's not that you actually have to ask your question (although, if there's an opportunity, it's a great way to practise speaking up with clarity and confidence). Instead, it's about making sure you're switched on – not only taking in the content, but actively absorbing and analysing it.

Stuck for ideas about what kind of question to ask? Here are a few easy tips:

- Think about how the content of the presentation relates to your real-life work experience. Have you been in a scenario in which the speaker's content is relevant? Did it work out in the same way as the speaker is describing? If not, why not? Were there practical implications that the speaker hasn't considered?

- Reflect on the past, or on the future. Think outside the present moment – can you ask a question about the history or evolution of the speaker's content? Can you ask a question about the future development of the topic?
- Cross-reference to other topics. Great ideas often come from comparisons or analogies between different topics, industries or areas of expertise. Can you reason by analogy to a different subject area, and make a comment about the speaker's content based on your comparison?
- Ask a question about the speaker. What led them to their interest in this particular topic? Do they encounter the same subject matter in their everyday work? Could they give an example of when they've seen the issues play out in practice?
- Draw on the speaker's content to go deeper. Start your question with a reference to something they've already been describing in the presentation. Then ask: could you say more about that?

2. Make notes – preferably on paper

A good sign of an engaged audience is a room full of note-takers. The simple act of inscribing content for future reference shows the speaker that you care enough to make the effort. It's also a great way to make sure you're learning as you go (especially if you can find the time to review your notes after the presentation). It also gives you a great way of locating material with which to craft a question (on which, see above).

Watch out, however, for note-taking on laptops or phones. If it's all you have available, go for it – but be aware that it can make you look disengaged, or like you have something more important to do. If you're using a laptop or phone, the best strategy is to write, then listen, then write.

3. Intentional eye contact

Eye contact with the speaker is a shortcut to being a valued audience member. Not only does it provide the speaker with the confidence to know that you're awake and listening in, but it also means you're much more likely to be focused on the content. Watch out, however, for making eye contact in a disconcerting, unbroken way – keep it natural, and switch it up with note-taking or looking at presentation materials.

Conference calls

Yes, they can be tedious, but learning to craft a conference call in a way that gets the job done with efficiency and ease will be a vital skill as a junior lawyer. The following are some suggestions for keeping the call on track, and for making life a little easier for all participants:

- Dial in early, if possible. And make sure you have a reliable line.
- The mute button is *always* your friend (unless you're speaking). Make it the first thing you use when you join the call.
- If you're leading the call, start at the appointed time, take a roll-call of who else has joined, and then set the agenda.
- If you have questions, make sure they're directed explicitly at the individual with the answers. Speak slowly, carefully and clearly. If you end up talking at the same time as someone else, stop, and wait for them to finish. If they continue to talk over you, try something like: 'When you're finished, I have a couple of points to make.'
- Keep the discussion on track by reminding the participants, where appropriate, how much time is left. If there are additional issues, follow up by email, or set up another specific call to deal with them. If possible, finishing early will (as ever) give people a positive recollection of the call.

Common mistakes

The mistake: not knowing when to stop

With smaller speaking roles – for example, during team meetings, feedback sessions or in a one-on-one context – know when you've said enough. As a general rule, speak for no longer than a couple of minutes without pausing or giving an opportunity for others to ask questions. Be aware of people shifting in their seats, or attempting to interject (in this situation: pause, take a breath, and ask them if they'd like to say something). You can always wrap up a segment with the phrase: 'Does anyone have any questions on what I've said so far?'

The mistake: fearing the nerves

Nerves are a natural part of public speaking – some studies suggested that people feared public speaking more than their own mortality! But nerves can also be harnessed for effective fuel, and knowing how to react in a high-adrenaline situation will give you the confidence to put yourself forward more often. Here's how to (constructively!) handle the nerves:

- Take a second. Make sure you have a couple of moments – alone, uninterrupted – before you head into the situation. Spend a few minutes reviewing your notes, and another few minutes focusing on your breath. If you can grab some fresh air, or take a short walk, you might find it helps to still your mind. Above all, however, it's important to walk into the room without immediate distractions – so avoid checking your phone, or your email, or starting a new discussion with someone just before your talk.

- Be overprepared. Spend longer than necessary in getting ready for your presentation. Have much more material than you're able to deliver. The knowledge of having deep, in-depth mastery of your topic will give you some much-needed reassurance when it comes to standing up in front of an audience.
- Remember why you're doing it. One of the best ways to get rid of nerves is to take yourself out of the picture: remember that you're doing it for the benefit of others. Any talk, presentation or speaking opportunity serves a specific purpose: to take the audience on a journey towards a new understanding. What do you want your audience to take away from your talk? How do you want to change their minds about the topic? By reframing the situation, it's much easier to think less about yourself and more about other people.
- Embrace the feeling. Think of nerves as a gift, making you more alert, more prepared and ready to face anything that comes your way. Nerves can remind you that you're not always playing it safe: that you're willing to take risks, and learn, and grow. See if you can sit with the nervous feelings – embrace them, even – and be grateful that you get to do something so important to you that it gives you butterflies.

The mistake: being boring (and what to do about it)

One of a speaker's worst fears is an audience full of people checking their email. And it's not because the speaker doesn't understand the temptation to pull out an iPhone. It's about something deeper than that: the fear that you are – whisper it – boring.

So, how to avoid being boring?

In the moment, practise reading the room – scan the space to see if you have people's attention. Listen to the responses of the audience: when do they laugh, or lean in, or look interested? When do they turn to the person next to them, or check their watch, or make notes?

Later, review your presentation: be honest with yourself about what resonated, and what didn't. And finally, check in with the audience. Ask for feedback (either by way of general email, or directly from a friendly individual). Get the specifics: which bits of content could have been cut? Which sections were a hit?

In need of a more immediate solution?

- Change your tone, pace, or movement. Grab people's attention back by switching to a faster – or slower – pace, standing up, moving towards the audience, or pausing altogether. If you've been droning on in the same tone for a while, a change in presentation style is likely to make people look up and re-engage.
- Make a light-hearted acknowledgement that the subject matter is fairly dry, and let people know why it's important: take them on the journey

with you. Your audience members will appreciate the personality that this admission brings, and they'll be glad to get a sense of the presentation's overall significance.

- Ask a question. Calling on specified individuals in the room can be effective – and might startle the audience into paying closer attention.
- Take a break. If the presentation time allows, get people to take a one-minute break to discuss a point with their neighbour, or to take notes.
- Show something different: break up long periods of verbal discussion with something else, whether it be visual, aural or physical. Showing an image or film, playing music, or even handing out materials (handouts, notes, props) can shake an audience awake.

Chapter 3

Communication: the unspoken word

Who you are within the world of work

This chapter is about your professional identity – all the messages you're communicating without saying a word. We'll cover the concept of a 'personal brand', the types of non-verbal communication (and how to master them), and the process of making a name for yourself in the office environment. We'll also look at developing expertise: figuring out what interests you most, and communicating it to others. This is hard work, but the rewards are significant and enduring. Let's get into it.

Define yourself

What is a personal brand?

The idea of a personal brand is simple: it's about developing and promoting yourself – and your career – as a marketer would develop and promote a brand. Your personal brand is the mix of experiences, personality and skills that make you unique. It's also your ticket to career success, a way to express your character, and the means to make an impact on the world, all rolled into one. Convinced? Read on for the details.

What is my personal brand? How do I find it?

Working through the checklist below will help you to identify your personal strengths, your purpose, your passion, and the background experience that makes you unique. Grab a sheet of paper or make notes on the space beneath the questions.

CHECKLIST 3.1: IDENTIFYING YOUR ANGLE

1. Let's start with your strengths. Think back to a time in the past where you've received great feedback for a piece of work or project. What was it that you were being congratulated on? Your writing style? Your commercial awareness? Your

organisational skills? Note down anything that seems relevant – and pay particular attention to anything that aligns with other pieces of feedback you've received.

2. Next, recall a piece of work or project that you felt great about – one that tapped into all of your abilities and challenged you to produce a successful outcome. What was it about the work that you enjoyed? Get specific: was it the nature of the work itself? The topic you were dealing with? The team you worked alongside? Make a note of anything you pick up.
3. Think about your purpose and passions (the two will often come together: it might be the case that you discover your passions as you pursue a greater purpose, or vice versa). If you're not sure you've found your purpose or passion yet, consider the following:

   - What do you want? Make a list of everything that comes to mind (and be honest). Go one step deeper. If you've noted down that you want career success, or a bigger salary, ask yourself: what *kind* of success do I want? Why do I want it? When would a certain salary be enough? Keep asking until you end up with a list of specific, identifiable items.
   - What gets you up in the morning? We all have a reason to keep going – even if it's buried somewhere deep down. Is it family? Community? A sense of curiosity about the world? Again, get specific – and be honest.
   - Which challenges in the world get you most passionate? Politics? Inequality? Justice? Is there an issue that makes you want to stand up and do something about it? Is there a cause that needs to be fought for? A problem that needs to be solved? Something – or someone – that needs your help?

   Look back through your answers to these questions, and identify common threads. Maybe there's a theme developing (don't worry if there isn't – just experiment with searching for connections). Maybe you're realising that there's way more to be passionate about than you previously thought.
4. Track your story – from the very beginning, all the way to the current moment. Make particular notes of the following:

   - any childhood experiences that shape the way you see the world;
   - any mentors, guides or teachers that opened your eyes to something; and
   - places in which you lived or worked that showed you a new culture, or a new way of life, or a new community.

   How did these experiences change you? How do you see things differently now? How did you choose to respond to things that happened to you?
5. Develop your story. What kind of personal brand do you want to take into your future? Can you think of people whose personal brands inspire you? How can you walk towards this as your career develops?
6. Final step: draw all of the threads together. Working back through your answers to the previous questions, look for common themes and overarching connections. Is there an area where your skills and abilities match up to the things you're most passionate about? Are there any similarities between the formative experiences of your life and the work you feel compelled to do in the world?

Take some time to think about it. At **Appendix A**, you'll find a template to help you put pen to paper and map out these ideas.

How does my personal brand work in practice?

Your personal brand will be reflected in a couple of tangible ways – most obviously, in your CV and your work biography. The work bio will usually be placed on your firm's website, or included in corporate materials when you attend pitches or presentations. In a less tangible sense, your personal brand feeds into everything you do – from interactions with colleagues, to formal pieces of work, to opportunities that come your way in the office. Your personal brand is how people begin to know you; the things they begin to associate you with.

Your personal brand is similar to your reputation – but it's more empowering than that. While your reputation is subject to the views and opinions of others, your personal brand is carefully developed, deliberately formed, and intentionally projected.

Here are some specific ways you'll be using your personal brand as you move through your career:

1. Opportunities

Choosing when to say 'yes' to things (and when to say 'no') is difficult – but the choice is much more clear when you know who you are and what you're doing. Does the opportunity align with your purpose and passions? Does it fit with the values you've cultivated for your personal brand? If not, you'll find it much easier to let it go. You have limited time and resources within your career – make sure they're spent with intention and integrity.

2. New positions

Whether internal or external, you'll probably be moving positions at some point. This might seem like a distant possibility during your years of training, but don't underestimate the speed at which you'll grow, develop and change. As you move through your training contract, becoming clearer and more certain about your personal brand will set you up with excellent foundations when the time comes to move onwards (and upwards).

3. Networking

If the word 'networking' makes you a little uncomfortable (more on that later – see **Chapter 7**), stick to the idea of simply 'meeting new people'. Whenever you meet someone, you're handing them an image of yourself – most likely before you've even opened your mouth. If you're clear on your personal brand – knowing who you are and what you're here to do – the impression you leave with others will also be clear. You're also much more likely to be memorable to someone: it's not often you encounter someone with clarity of purpose, skills and intent (especially during the junior years of their career).

What's not being said

You've probably heard it before, but it's worth repeating: in general, the impression you leave with others is not based on the words you say. You may have heard about the 55-38-7 rule, which breaks down communication. According to this rule, 55 per cent of communication is body language, and 38 per cent is tone of voice. Only 7 per cent comes down to the words actually spoken. While the breakdown of percentages is not an exact science, and of the application of the rule is nuanced, the point remains clear. *What* you say doesn't matter nearly as much as *how* you say it (and the intention *behind* the words).

Let's work through two basic questions in the area of non-verbal communication. Firstly, how can you learn to observe the non-verbal communication of others? And, secondly, how can you learn to improve your own non-verbal communication so that you're able to deliver a controlled, effective message?

Understanding others

- Begin by being fully present with the other person. Put your phone away, remove any other immediate distractions and start to pay close attention. Be aware of their eye contact and subtle movements – do these cues match your interpretation of the situation? Is there anything in the other person's behaviour that stands out to you?
- What about the tone of the other person? The pace of their speech? The pitch and volume of their voice? Are they stumbling? Murmuring? Repeating the same thing over and over?
- Are there any noticeable gestures in the other person's communication? How are they using their hands (if at all)? How much space do they seem comfortable taking up? What kind of impression would they be giving if you were simply observing them, without any sound?

Understanding yourself

- Observe yourself in communication as if you were watching from someone else's perspective. What kind of posture are you adopting? Are your arms folded, or legs crossed? Are you leaning forwards, or slouching? Subtle cues from a person's body language can give a powerful message: take a quick scan of your own position to make sure you know what's going on.

- Are you fully present in your current location, or have you brought any emotions, history or other feelings with you? It's easy – and natural – to carry around the accumulated psychological baggage of the day (the irritation you felt on your commute, for example, or the dissatisfaction of a bad morning). But try to be aware of it: analyse yourself, and see if you can set aside all other feelings and emotions. You can (and probably should) work through those experiences later, but – for now – practise being fully present in *this* moment.
- Watch out for any impulsive reactions to situations. Research has shown that we develop our instinctive patterns of thought and behaviour through sustained repetition. However, we also have the power to break out of it. Catch yourself responding to situations in undesirably predictable ways, and note down the cause and the response. The next time the same situation arises, challenge yourself to choose a different reaction. Begin to rewire your brain: create new neurological pathways (which can, eventually, create better outcomes for yourself).

Exploring your expertise

What is your expertise?

In this section, we'll assume that 'expertise' refers to the things you're best at: your specialism; the skills that set you apart from others. Your expertise is the thing that makes you unique in your workplace. It doesn't have to be a specific area of practice: it could be your presentation skills, your drafting style, or your project management abilities. Your specialism may change over time (this is normal and to be expected), and you may not have any idea what it is yet (again – this is both normal and fully expected). This section aims to get you thinking about what that area of expertise might be, and – once you've identified it – how you can go about developing it.

To get started, ask yourself the following questions:

- Which pieces of work have received the best feedback during your time in the workplace?
- Which pieces of work have you felt like resulted in the most (or most rapid) personal growth for you?
- Are there any areas in which you seemed to advance faster than your peers or colleagues?
- Are there any skills or abilities that come easily to you, where you can see that others may struggle?
- What do you love to do? When do you lose yourself in a sense of 'flow' in the workplace?

- What do others know you for in the office? Do you have a reputation for being good at a particular skill, task or project?
- Have you had a strong capability or passion for something since childhood, that now shows up in your work?

Make some notes on your answers (you can also revisit the previous section on personal branding to pick out some overarching themes and commonalities). In **Appendix A**, you'll find some examples of structures that you can play around with when working through your answers.

It might also be helpful to go through the questions with another trainee or colleague – take turns to ask each other the questions, and discuss your thoughts. It could be the case that you're too immersed in the details of your life to see the 'bigger picture', and other people's reflections can be of great help.

Are you fixed, or are you evolving?

Let's assume you've got an answer to the questions above, and you're pretty clear about what your expertise is – at least, for the time being (it's not a problem if you're still not sure – you can always pick something just to try out the next exercise). What are you supposed to do next?

Take a step back. There are a couple of ways to look at your career. One is from a fixed perspective: you follow the structured hierarchy of your organisation; you allow your interests to be guided and shaped by your supervisors; you end up in a particular area of practice just because it was available, or because it seemed easy, or because someone told you that you should do it.

Alternatively, you can choose to reframe things. Instead of a fixed, rigid progression, you can choose to see your career as an evolving pathway – a pathway that you shape, with intention, as you walk it. You can choose to see your work as a cultivated expression of personal interest; a reflection of the growth and development that you've worked to achieve; an individual path that is fully and uniquely yours.

The fixed perspective takes much less effort, that's for sure. However, the evolving perspective is where true enjoyment lies, and where the foundations for a sustainable, fulfilling career are laid.

How do you evolve within an organisation?

We'll start with a story.

Imagine a trainee solicitor who has just started her first seat in a high street law firm – let's call her Emily. Emily was interested in family law when she was a student, and studied the topic at university. In particular, she's interested in matrimonial disputes. Her first two seats are in other areas, but in her third seat – finally! – she's in the family department. What could she do to start building her expertise – and expressing her developing interest – in this area of practice?

The main way (of course) is to do the work that she is assigned by her supervisor, and do it to an excellent standard (for help with this, see the first couple of chapters on communication). However, there are other opportunities for her to start building her brand. Here are some examples.

1. Become an expert, even in a very small way

As a trainee, the easiest way of developing expertise is to pick up (and master) topics that are new to everyone in your workplace. This is most likely to be a piece of new legislation, but it could also be a new case that changes existing practice, or a new set of government proposals. Emily could keep on top of all new developments and legal changes during her seat, and volunteer to read up on them when they arise. This, in turn, can lead to opportunities such as:

- talks and presentations;
- internal (or external) training sessions;
- articles, blogs and other publications;
- writing for internal training or know-how materials;
- briefing other lawyers – whether junior or senior – on the topic; and/or
- attending (or even presenting at) conferences of interest.

Eventually, Emily's name will get known throughout her firm as someone who is knowledgeable about the particular topic. This is *especially* likely to be the case if Emily actively pushes herself forwards, and volunteers for things like presentations or writing articles (and promotes or pitches them herself, even if no one else has taken the initiative and actually asked her).

2. Use the expertise around you to your maximum ability

Most trainees see their supervisor primarily as a source of work (and perhaps as a source to be consulted with a research-related question, when all other options are exhausted). Very few trainees see their supervisor as someone who can easily – if asked – accelerate their own growth curve far beyond what would normally be expected in a six-month seat rotation.

If Emily approaches her supervisor-trainee relationship as if she were in an academic learning environment – working to make sure she asks intelligent questions, and being fully receptive to the answers she receives – it's likely she'll come away with a lot more than trainees who have sat in the same seat before her. Developing this attitude will also get her name known in the department as someone who is driven, intellectually curious and ready to learn – all good groundwork for the expansion of her expertise in that area of practice.

3. Talk to other people about what you want to do; ask their advice

Broadening the circle from the immediate trainee-supervisor connection, Emily can also look around the department for advice. She can start out with the other junior lawyers in the team: tracking back from their current positions, she should be able to work out how they got there – which seats they did, how they got their positions, what they've specialised in. She can reach out directly: drop them an email, ask them if they have time for lunch or coffee, prepare an informal list of questions to discuss. She'll find – as is nearly always the case – that people are more than willing to discuss their experiences with their junior colleagues. They'll often have a whole range of tips, guidance and advice (which will have the benefit of being tried and tested through experience!).

What about developing expertise post-qualification?

Back to Emily. Let's assume she got her place in her desired department, and has been busy using all the steps above to develop her expertise up to this point. What next? Is there anything she should bear in mind after reaching qualification?

1. Stay interested

Staying interested: it sounds obvious, but it's not always straightforward. On qualification, it's easy to slip into complacency about your area of practice. It's easy to get caught up in the daily workload and the pressures that come with your new position. It's easy to forget why you wanted to do it in the first place. Here are a few ways to set up the habits, practices and routines that allow you to stay interested in what you do.

- **Subscribe to news updates for your area of practice.** Start by asking members of your team (and your supervisor) for recommendations. Which resources do they read regularly? Which publications are worth your attention? How regularly should you be checking relevant update emails? Gather the wisdom of others, and craft your own regular intake of content.

  Next, get into the habit of reading and reviewing the information. It's fine (and helpful) simply to be up to date with what's going on, but attempt to be proactive with your new understanding: use the information to open up discussions with supervisors, or learn enough about a topical matter to be able to teach others.
- **Track your progress in a professional development journal**. We'll get to the topic of professional development journals and trackers in **Chapter 4**, but for now, just consider ways in which you can track and capture your progress. Can you create a know-how document for yourself, in which you record links, resources and pieces of information? Can you

keep a journal on hand in which to note down relevant updates, or topics you want to learn more about?

Research indicates that you don't even need to come back and review your notes for this method to be effective. Just the simple act of intentionally recording information will help to cement it in your mind.

- **Look for conferences and trainings to attend.** Sign up for the updates in your field: conferences; online trainings; industry briefings. When you find something relevant (and which looks like it has practical application for your area of practice), run it past your team and supervisor. Make your pitch: why are you interested in attending it? What additional knowledge or awareness would it bring to the group as a whole? How will you capitalise on that knowledge – will you, for example, be taking notes throughout and circulate a summary afterwards? Will you undertake to give a debrief or short presentation on what you learned?
- **Take all opportunities to talk about your work with junior lawyers.** This includes trainees, vacation schemers, open day students, and aspiring law students. Any time you're presented with an opportunity to discuss your practice area with others, grab it with both hands. Not only will it enhance your own understanding of what you do, but you're also more likely to develop a genuine passion for the topic if you can use your knowledge to inspire others. Step into roles of mentoring and informal coaching for junior members of your team, or for vacation scheme students. You'll be surprised at the energy and enthusiasm that it will bring to your own experience. You are also far more likely to discover the real reasons behind why you're doing the work you do (if you've never articulated it, it's easy to skim over it). Talking to other lawyers, especially at the more junior side of the profession, can help to clarify and strengthen your own understanding of the ways you've progressed (and continue to progress) in your career.

2. Set up your networks

Starting to build early relationships within your firm (and even externally) will be greatly beneficial to you in the long term. Reach out to senior people and ask them questions: about their career, about their area of practice, about their expertise and interests. Ask them for pieces of advice they would hand down to junior lawyers. Ask them for opportunities to get involved in projects that sound interesting. You'll be surprised at how this effort compounds over time: investing in your relationships is one of the most effective ways to establish solid career foundations.

For more on networks, mentors and mentoring, see **Chapters 6** and **7**.

3. Seek out leadership opportunities

One of the most important distinguishing features between trainee and junior lawyer is the ability to lead others. As you move up towards associate-level work, you'll also move towards a different place within the team, and you're likely to have trainees (and perhaps paralegals, or legal secretaries) assisting you. If you end up with one of these situations on your hands as a trainee, lean into it. Learning these skills early on will set you up for success when you move into more formal positions of leadership in future. Bear in mind the following points:

- Communication skills are, of course, essential to your success as a junior leader. Revisit **Chapters 1** and **2** to fine-tune the essentials.
- Enthusiasm, passion and genuine interest in others will take you a long way. Cultivate a sense of curiosity about the work of others within your team. Ask them questions (and actually listen to their responses). You'll be surprised at how willing people are to follow leaders who evidently have their best interests at heart.
- Observe without judgment. Part of becoming a great leader is the understanding of how – and why – people operate in certain ways within the workplace. See if you can spot patterns of behaviour, or strengths and weaknesses of your team members. Start to understand your team beyond a superficial level. Don't expect perfection here – people (and teams) are immensely complex, after all. Just make a consistent commitment to enhancing your understanding.
- Lead the way by example. Most effective leaders are appealing because they model an example of something we want. If you're promoting a certain ideal – perhaps of an efficient, commercially focused solicitor – make sure you live up to the standards that you set for yourself. Again, it's not about being perfect. It's about the importance of being genuine, standing behind what you publicly promote, and putting the effort into ongoing self-development.

4. Be proactive; get involved

Keep your eyes open: look for chances to step up and help out. If there's an opportunity to volunteer for a project that interests you, take it. If there's a client-related meeting or conference call happening, ask if you can attend and take notes. Suggest ideas, if you have them. Integrate and apply the knowledge that you have about a particular area or field of law. Move projects forwards: if you can suggest a next step, do so. Keep your team members motivated. Speak up at meetings. Watch your mentors and peers and observe the way they move through their career paths.

You don't have to do it all at once, of course. Instead, choose the tactics that work for you, and start to experiment with them in your day-to-day working life. It might also help to keep a note of the things that seem to be most successful.

5. Seek (and respond to) feedback

A large part of finding your initial career foundations will determined by your ability to receive and respond to feedback. Yes, it's uncomfortable – no one likes to hear a piece of criticism about themselves (even if it is phrased 'constructively'). It's easy to lapse into a lazy view of feedback: the view that you are a passive recipient of information.

It takes a lot of intentional effort – and a significant degree of skill – to flip your feedback mindset entirely, so that each piece of feedback becomes a valuable tool for your professional and personal growth. But it *is* possible – and it's worth it. Start with the basics, and think about the overall structure of a feedback session. The list below will give you an overview (plus some tips and tricks) – for a more detailed checklist, see **Chapter 4**.

- **Before it begins.** This is the time to set your expectations. Check yourself for any emotions or instinctive defensiveness that begins to kick in. Get yourself back to a position of neutrality, ready to receive the information in its purest form. And take a notebook in with you – it'll be far easier to record exactly what was said in the moment, rather than waiting to dredge up your recollections later.
- **During the meeting.** Take in the information that's presented to you (and take it down in the form of brief notes). Ask questions about what went well, what could have been improved, and how you could do things differently next time. If you feel like you want to add additional background information of your own, do so – but make sure you don't come across as if you're trying to absolve yourself of responsibility. The feedback session should be a two-way process, but keep the conversation factual – watch out for attribution of blame, or discussion of personal characteristics, or feelings of irritation, anxiety or annoyance. You can unpack all the details later, but for now – just receive it.
- **After the meeting.** This is the time to revisit your notes. Add in any personal observations and pointers on how to improve things for the next time. Approach the feedback from a place of self-development. How can you use the information to improve? How could the content be used as a tool to accelerate your professional growth?

It's important to remember, of course, that feedback shouldn't be taken as fact without further analysis. It may be that the person giving feedback isn't well trained in the skill of delivery, or they may be missing crucial information that shapes the information you receive. Use your own judgment:

decide what to incorporate and what to discard. Be honest with yourself – try and leave any sense of personal pride or ego to the side.

Finally, make sure you end up with a couple of practical action points. While all feedback is useful (even if only to give you another perspective on your work), its real utility will come when you're able to put it into practice. Can you turn statements into suggestions for how to improve? Can you redraft reflections from your experience into specific things to do (or not do) next time?

For more on feedback, see **Chapter 4**.

Common mistakes

The mistake: inauthenticity

This is, perhaps, the biggest danger of developing the different forms of unspoken communication. Authenticity will look different on everyone, but it's crucial to remain connected to your truest personality, opinions and emotions. You may think no one will notice if you fake an office persona for yourself, but it often spills out in hundreds of subtle ways (and, most importantly, it will make your working life miserable).

Check in with yourself as you go about the difficult work of developing a personal brand and exploring your expertise. Wherever you end up, make sure it feels like a natural fit. Journalling exercises, sessions with mentors and professional development tracking can all help you to stick to your path (for more on all of this, see **Chapter 4**).

The mistake: body language

There are several obvious (but easily overlooked) things to watch out for with your body language. Scan the list below, and work to avoid them in the future:

- **Posture and stance.** Watch out for 'closed' body language: arms folded; body positioned away from others; legs crossed. Ideally, you want to come across as natural and relaxed. Try softening the muscles in your shoulders, or standing with your feet planted firmly and legs uncrossed. You can double-check your posture in a mirror – it's always helpful to know what it looks like from the outside.
- **Fidgeting.** Best to just avoid this entirely (at least, in public). Fidgeting generally makes you come across as nervous, anxious or distracted. The main habits to look out for are: nail-biting, lip-biting, hair-playing, playing with jewellery or watches, and an inability to sit still. It's easier to work on these habits if you don't see them as something 'bad' that you have to discipline yourself out of: instead, just notice them when they arrive, and then calmly turn your attention towards becoming still.

- **Leaning in; leaning out.** Closely linked to posture and stance is the use of your body in space – and in relation to the space of others. Leaning in (at an appropriate point in time, and keeping an appropriate distance) when someone is speaking can be incredibly effective. Leaning out can have the same impact when someone is finished speaking: it can convey a period of reflection, or an emotion brought on by the speaker. Again, none of these are rules set in stone: play with the techniques, and see what works for you.
- **Eye contact.** Long, intentional eye contact gives the impression of confidence and self-assurance. Just don't make it so long as to be creepy – give the other person an opportunity to break your gaze, and avoid being both wide-eyed and unblinking.
- **Handshakes.** Firm, calm and well-practised is best. Ask a friend or family member to try it out with you – you'll only get better by receiving feedback (even for something as seemingly trivial as a handshake). Whatever you're doing, take ownership of it – nothing worse than an apologetic handshaker with a weak grip and fumbling grasp.
- **Distance and space.** Encroaching on another person's personal space might be one of the worst body language offences. Read the people you're with: are they frequently leaning away from you, or stepping back? If so, back off – give them space. Standing at a distance and speaking without force can – if executed well – draw people towards you. Think about the impression you want to give, and then (as with pretty much everything else) practise, and keep practising.

The mistake: deprioritising the intangibles

It's tempting to put things like 'personal branding' to one side, in favour of more immediate work (or non-work) activities with a tangible result, but the *intangible* work you do on yourself will be the stuff that really results in a return on investment in the future.

Staying focused and accountable to yourself will help: consider setting up a regular time or date to check in with yourself and map out your progress. Watching your development over time (and perhaps looking to the progress of peers or colleagues as a helpful benchmark) could be the inspiration and fuel you need to continue on the journey of personal growth and evolution.

Chapter 4

Professional development

Navigating the start of your legal career

You've probably heard it before: self-improvement is the key to sustainable, long-term growth throughout your career. In fact, this is not just about your training contract, or even about the first couple of years as a junior lawyer. This is about setting the foundations for a long career of evolution, progression and achievement. Convinced? This chapter will cover the basics of your professional development – we'll cover personal development in the next chapter.

Taking ownership of your career

Let's focus on your supervisor, or a senior lawyer at your firm. Think back to the time when they were entering the legal profession. In previous years, employees often had their career paths mapped out for them – you've probably heard of phrases like 'a job for life' or being on 'partnership track' from a junior level.

Things are different now. With the rise of the portfolio career, later retirement ages, and the rapid disruption and reformation of numerous industries, we can no longer sit back and relax into a pre-determined career template. Today's junior lawyers must learn the art of self-development, and chart their course for themselves.

There are, of course, plenty of reasons why this is a positive change. Yes, it involves more work, and it might seem more uncertain – but it also allows you to shape and form the career you end up with. It ensures you don't sleepwalk through your working life, allowing outside forces to make decisions about your specialism and progression and job description. In short, it allows you to take ownership.

Why is ownership a good thing? Well, research indicates that employees who feel more in control of the evolving path of their career feel more fulfilled and motivated, on average, than others. You're also much less likely to experience feelings of resentment or irritation towards your working environment: if *you* get to choose where you're headed, the direction (and responsibility) is in your hands.

Why track your professional growth?

To begin, here are a few reasons why this chapter is worth your time, starting with the very first day of your career.

1. You'll discover what it is you really want

The act of methodically recording your ambitions, goals and reflections will, over time, develop into a picture of who you are at work, and who you want to be. This kind of information will be invaluable to you in your years as a junior lawyer, as you begin to make career-defining choices (practice area specialisation, for example). Committing to a mechanism for tracking your own development during this time is a priceless investment in your future growth.

2. You start to see the wood (as well as the trees)

Have you ever felt like you were lost in the day-to-day, so immersed in the details that you lose sight of the bigger picture? Let's admit it – this happens to all of us. It's only natural: we need to focus on the detail of the task at hand, and absorb ourselves in the day ahead. This allows us to function efficiently, prioritise, take action and make progress. This is great – but as a by-product, we often forget to take a step back and look at things with a wider lens. In the proverbial sense, we struggle to see the wood for the trees.

When you reflect on your progress over the last month, or last quarter, or last year, you'll be staggered at the rate of growth (this is especially true as a junior lawyer, when you're just beginning). However, looking back over the past week alone might give you a totally different picture. Chances are, the things that seem like game-changers in the past week (a nervous encounter with a supervisor; an error in a document; a piece of encouraging feedback) will fit into a much broader picture when you slot them in alongside 12 previous weeks of equivalent details. Tracking your development helps you do just that: you'll learn to read the overall curve of your working life, as opposed to making judgments based on specific situations, or on individual moments in time.

3. You'll work on your ability to focus, to be patient, and to learn from your own experiences

Focus will come with a newly aligned and orientated set of goals, and from the sense of achievement that dedicated development tracking will bring you. *Patience* will grow over weeks of commitment to your chosen tracking mechanism. *Learning* from your own experiences will happen when you begin to reflect and restructure your working life in line with your findings from self-analysis.

Research has indicated that professional development journalling can give rise to more clarity, optimism and attention. This effect, by the way, was evident even in those who performed no more than 10 minutes a day of brief reflection on their working lives. That's probably less time than you spend flicking through social media on a coffee break.

On board with the idea? Let's break down some of the main tools available.

Main tools available

Professional development journal

Otherwise known as a 'work diary', this simple tracking tool will allow you to record, reassess and realign your working behaviour in order to achieve great results. Start by getting hold of a journal. It doesn't have to be anything special: any notebook will work. Something with a cover, though: make it easily identifiable and not visible to others when closed.

Next, set yourself a dedicated time to complete the work. Around 10 minutes every day (or every other day, but keep it regular) should work well. Finding a regular place can also be helpful – perhaps a favourite coffee shop, or on the commute home. It will be even more helpful if you can consistently complete this work out of the office: the switch in environment will give you some much-needed distance (in both the physical and psychological sense).

So, you have the materials, and you have the time and space. What should you be writing? Here's a quick checklist to work through, although you can – and should! – expand this with your own ideas, and develop it as you continue to do the work over a period of months or years. Remember that these are just suggestions, and you should craft the tools that work best for you.

CHECKLIST 4.1: PROFESSIONAL DEVELOPMENT JOURNAL

1. Open the page by recording the date you're making the entry.
2. Get it all out: write it down in a free-flowing, stream-of-consciousness style. Write anything that comes to mind about the day (or days) since you wrote the previous entry. Take up some space, and don't be afraid to spend some time on this section. The point is not to read it back and critically analyse what you've written; the exercise is much more about clearing your mind in preparation for some focused reflection.
3. After you've worked through your free-flow writing exercise, answer the following questions (feel free, of course, to add your own!):
    - What am I most excited about at work at the moment? Why? How can I take steps to incorporate more things like this into my working life?

- What am I least excited about at work at the moment? Why? Are there any steps I can take to shape the experience into something positive? What does the experience have to teach me?
- In general, how I am I feeling about work today? Perhaps give yourself a ranking out of 10 (and include a short note to explain why).
- Who have I helped at work today? Who has helped me most at work today?
- What (or who) do I feel most grateful for today, within my working environment?

4. Next up, check in with your goals and ambitions. It might be helpful to copy these into the front page of your professional development journal, so you have them to hand. Have you taken a step (tiny, almost-imperceptible steps still count!) towards your goals? How? If not, why not? How could you do things differently tomorrow? Are your goals still the right ones for you? If not, how do they need to be shaped in line with your current priorities?
5. Feedback. If you're not using a specific feedback tracker (on which, see below), consider incorporating a feedback element into your professional development journal. Have you received any feedback today? Do you, on reflection, consider it to be constructive and helpful for your personal growth? What can you learn from it? How will your behaviour change in response to it? Did you give any feedback to others? How did it help (or not) the situation? Will you do things differently next time (and if so, how)?
6. Any advice, learnings or things to take forwards? Things to remember? Things to avoid? Pieces of wisdom handed down to you? Put these items in a separate section, marked out on the page so that they are easily identifiable in future.
7. Finish up with a brief review of your notes, and of your notes from the previous couple of sessions. Pick out any major themes, narratives or developments. Look for consistencies and recurring items – and ask yourself what you can learn from them.

Feedback tracking and formal reviews

Along with a professional development journal, it's worth finding a method of capturing feedback that works well for you. Again, the form can be simple – any notebook will work – but it's worth keeping one separate from other journals. This way, you'll easily be able to identify past pieces of feedback, and observe a more accurate picture of your working life over time.

What kind of feedback should you be capturing? Well, anything and everything – the more you can record, the better. Even an off-handed comment after you turn in a piece of work for review can help you identify things to work on, or things you've done well. Get into the habit of noticing when someone hands over information about your work: it might not always be in a formal face-to-face meeting. Think about any feedback you receive over email, or things you hear from colleagues, or subtle comments mentioned during team meetings.

All of these things matter – in fact, informal pieces of feedback are likely to be just as helpful as formal reviews, as they often reveal what the individual *really* thinks (without having had time to reflect and articulate). However, for the big ones – the mid-year or end-of-year review – you'll want to go through a more detailed process.

Formal review sessions: a step-by-step guide

Formal review sessions will be a large part of the feedback you receive, and you should use them to your full advantage. Get yourself prepared before the meeting: know what to expect (who will be there? What will be discussed? How long will the meeting take?) and go in prepared (take a notebook and a set of questions to ask about your own development). It helps to spend some time working through your goals and ambitions, and comparing them to the work you've done since your last review. What worked? What didn't work? How much progress have you made?

If your firm makes any feedback available before the meeting, work carefully through it – highlight any positives you'd like to emphasise, and flag any negative feedback for discussion (if appropriate). If you don't get a preview into the content of the meeting, use the structure from previous reviews, or ask a colleague to describe what normally happens. Having a rough sense of what's up ahead will (help to) get rid of those pre-meeting nerves.

When you're in the meeting itself, take notes (lots of them). It doesn't matter if you're taking them down in stream-of-consciousness style: you'll have time to refine later. For now, what matters most is that you capture all of it – it's not necessarily the case that what you think to be important in the context of the meeting will still be as important when you come to reanalyse your notes.

Make sure you ask questions, too – clarify anything that seems unclear; dig deeper if you feel like a point hasn't been fully expressed; make broader enquiries about your own development.

Bring the attention of the reviewer to things that have gone well, even if they don't bring it up themselves. Most supervisors will naturally balance the positives and negatives, giving you a holistic sense of your performance – but if they don't do it, fight for yourself. Drawing out your own successes is a skill – very different from bragging or boasting about your achievements – and it's one you can develop. Make sure you know which successes you want to emphasise, and why (think about your personal brand, and the kind of reputation you'd like to cultivate). Back up each assertion with evidence. Adding some positive things about your relationship with your supervisor or other senior team members will also be helpful. Remember that your review is as much about personality and cultural fit as it is about billable hours.

Leave the session with some tangible goals and action plans for the coming months. Know when your next review session will be, and what your supervisor expects you to have achieved by then. If there's something you want to add to close the conversation, take the chance – thank your supervisor for opportunities to work on projects you enjoyed, ask any final questions, or clarify the outcome of the discussion.

After the review has completed, use your notes to record the feedback in a more structured way. Highlight positives and negatives, and turn them into actionable steps. Keep them somewhere nearby, and refer back to them – perhaps at the end of every week, as you leave the office. Add (in a distinguishable colour, or on a separate page) pieces of informal feedback you collect as you move through the following months. Before your next review session, schedule yourself an hour or so to refresh your memory, and set yourself up to exceed your supervisor's expectations!

Cheat sheets, FAQ folders, curiosity lists

Looking for more ways to cement your knowledge, advance your skills and accelerate your professional development? This section covers a few other options. A word of warning to begin: these tools only work if you commit to using them regularly. However, the dedication will pay off – an investment of time and effort in the short term will pave the way for a much more efficient learning process in the long term.

Cheat sheets

You might remember this term from your studies – the cheat sheet is a one-page document that summarises, in practical terms, everything you need to know about a certain topic. The idea is to collate all relevant information in one place, and have it available whenever you work on a relevant task. The document can contain whatever information you find most useful: the only rules are that it should be a single page (hence the 'sheet' reference) and should provide a shortcut to avoid you having to look up the information afresh each time (hence the 'cheat' element).

For inspiration on designing your own cheat sheet, check out the example in **Appendix B** of this book.

FAQ folders

We've all been there: you've looked up the answer to a question or point of law a hundred times, and yet, when someone puts you on the spot, your mind has (helpfully) forgotten all the information. This is where your FAQ folder can come in useful.

Start by collecting answers to frequently asked questions during the first couple of months of your training contract. The questions could be anything from substantive points of law, to administrative details about booking cabs, conference rooms and taking days off. Store them somewhere (it doesn't have to be in hard copy – it could just as helpfully be a folder in your emails or on your desktop. What matters is that you remember to use it, and keep referring back to it).

As you begin to fill the folder with the answers to your own FAQs, try this: every time you include a new topic or answer to a question, refer back to the ones you have in there already. You don't have to intentionally 'revise' them, but make an effort to scan their content, and make sure you know they're in there somewhere. The next time the question arises, you're much more likely to go straight to the right place for the answer.

Your FAQ folder can also include questions: a list of things that you want to run past a supervisor when you have the chance, or questions to ask at the end of a deal or to look up when you have a quiet afternoon. Again, the important thing is not the format or the specific content of the folder: it's about intentionally setting up the learning and development systems that work for you (and having the commitment to stick to them).

Curiosity lists

Cultivating curiosity will be one of your most valuable skills as a junior lawyer. At a time when it's easy to surrender to overwhelm and work-related stress, your passion and genuine interest in practising law may be the things that keep you balanced and driven. Curiosity doesn't always just fall into your lap, however. You can develop a deeper, inquisitive passion by intentionally and deliberately searching it out. Here's how.

- An obvious one to start: get to know the basics of your area of practice. This will, of course, come over time, but make the most of any 'new joiner' materials you're given and any handover discussions that you have with previous trainees or supervisor.
- Read about your area of practice, and not just in a passive way: read with the intent to discover something new. When you do discover something, ask yourself why it might be interesting. Is it a new point of law you hadn't previously considered? Is it something that you haven't yet seen in practice? When you come across something that fascinates you, delve deeper. Read more; find someone who knows something about it; bring it up with your colleagues.
- If you don't have time to look into something right away, keep a running list of all the topics you'd like to know more about. Next time you have a (relatively) quiet moment in the office, pull up the list, flick through it, and find something that you can spend some time learning about. Developing your own small projects will not only advance your

awareness about certain areas of law, but it will also enhance your independent research skills (and fire up that sense of genuine curiosity at the same time).

Setting up a working CV

Think about your latest CV. It's probably set up in a perfect way to land you that training contract, vacation scheme or open day. Chances are, once you completed your job application process, you didn't give it a second thought. Why should you keep an updated CV once you've got yourself a job – right? Well, while that may be true (it's not essential to keep it updated when you're happy and settled in your current job), it's still worth your time to maintain a working CV document. This is why:

1. Updating your CV shows you the skills and abilities you're developing, while you're developing them. This is helpful – not just because you can track your own professional development, but because it gives you an overview of the kind of lawyer you're becoming (and this feeds into your personal brand, as well as enabling you to make changes to suit your goals and ambitions).
2. Keeping an up-to-date CV is always useful for any 'extra-curricular' activities you might be interested in (for example, going in to speak to other law students, or taking on charity positions). It's also an easy shortcut to producing a personal biography (which is often required for things like firm websites, pitches, presentations and articles).
3. Finally, of course – and just in case! – if you do need to look around for other opportunities (whether at the end of your training contract or otherwise), you'll have a carefully prepared, updated CV ready to go – whenever you need it.

Updating your CV, in this context, doesn't necessarily mean it must be perfect. It doesn't even have to be ready for external circulation. To make it as easy as possible for yourself, perhaps set up two documents: one is your 'circulation CV' (to be sent out to anyone who needs a copy) and the other is your 'working CV' (a work in progress, basically). In your working copy, use bullet-points, notes and shorthand – whatever works to record information about your achievements quickly and reliably. That way, you make sure you don't miss anything (and your future self will be incredibly grateful that you took the time to prepare).

Setting your own deadlines

Let's talk about deadlines. As junior lawyers, you're likely to be passed a deadline from a senior colleague (or, if you're working with clients directly, from the client themselves). Deadlines are one of the most stressful elements of life as a junior lawyer – so it's essential to know how to handle them. Here are several pointers to consider:

1. First up, get clear on your external deadline. What's the absolute latest date that the work needs to be done by? Make sure it's clear: if you have a vague deadline (for example: 'towards the end of the week'), clarify – and do it as soon as possible. Better to ask until you get an answer than be surprised with a deadline sooner than you'd anticipated.
2. Once you have your external deadline, work backwards. How much time do you anticipate you'll need for the task? For this process (which, let's be honest, is almost guesswork the first couple of times you perform a given task), compare the work to other similar tasks that you've previously done, or ask your supervisor how much time they think you should be spending.
3. Factor in additional time for any reliance you're placing on other people – are you asking a paralegal or secretary to help? Have you communicated your deadline to them (making sure you let them know your personal deadlines, and not just your supervisor's final deadline)? Are you waiting on external filings, or for something to be delivered, or for someone else to send you a document? Make sure you give yourself enough time for emergency scenarios – ideally, you want to have a buffer in which things could wrong (and be fixed).
4. Once you've set your deadlines, and start to get on with the work, keep yourself on track. Periodically check your calendar to make sure things are progressing in line with your deadline, and check in with other team members to make sure they feel the same way. Consistent, good-quality communication can save you from most deadline-related panics: if you're supervising other people (as well as being supervised yourself), make sure you facilitate it.

Project checklists

The start and the end of big projects are the best times to get yourself fully organised: at the start, to prepare for the work ahead; at the end, to reflect and learn from the project. Checklists are a great way of supporting this process: using them consistently at the start and the end of a matter will help you stay on top of workflow, prioritise, plan and take giant steps forwards in your progression as a lawyer.

To give you a sense of the types of things you can incorporate into your checklists, see below (remember that these are suggestions, and you should actively amend and adapt them to your personal requirements).

CHECKLIST 4.2: AT THE START OF A PROJECT

1. **The team.** Make sure you know the others who'll be working alongside you. Who is supervising you? Do you have all of their contact details to hand? Do you know their working hours and their office location? Who else is on the team? Will there be anyone for you to supervise?
2. **The background.** Will there be an opportunity to sit down with the team and talk through the background to the project? Will you have a chance to meet or discuss initial steps with the client? If not, will there be correspondence shared that you can use to get up to speed? Make sure you know how things are going to get started – you don't want to be on the back foot before things have even kicked off.
3. **The process.** Do you have a sense of how the project will develop? Any essential deadlines or important milestones you need to note? Ensure everything is diarised and recorded, where appropriate.
4. **The client.** Do you have all the background you need about this particular client? Anything you should be aware of in terms of expectations, process or work product? Could you check in with others who regularly do similar work for the same client, as well as your main supervisor for the project?
5. **Your toolkit.** Do you know what you need to get started? Any precedents, forms or guidance you should have to hand? Any previous projects that might provide a starting point, or resources that you know will be helpful? Assemble your toolkit and get it set up.
6. **Performance goals.** On a personal level, what do you want to achieve from the project? How will your success be measured? Do you know what you should do to stand out? Any personal skills, objectives or ambitions you want to achieve?
7. **Potential risks.** Sounds a bit pessimistic, but it's worth taking some time to work out the main things that could go wrong. Can you foresee deadline issues, or potential miscommunications, or a mismatch of expectations? By setting yourself up to see what could go wrong, you're much more likely to be able to map your way out of that situation in advance.

CHECKLIST 4.3: THE END OF A PROJECT

1. **Feedback and appraisals.** How did it go? How will success be measured? When will you get the opportunity to discuss the project with your supervisor? How will you know what the client thought of your performance? If the answers to these questions aren't yet obvious, set out the steps you need to get there.
2. **Things to take forwards.** What were the main learnings from the project? What do you want to take forwards? Is there anything you want others to know, or anything you want to remember for next time? Make a note of any significant lessons learned, or useful resources that should be revisited. If the project documents would serve as helpful precedents for future, follow your office procedures to make sure they're filed appropriately.
3. **Relationship-building.** Did you leave the project on a positive note? Is there an opportunity to thank the client for the ability to work on their project? Did you get a chance to express thanks to the rest of your team for their help, and for providing you

with a learning experience? The ability to reflect and express gratitude is often overlooked, but can be a powerful tool to make you stand out from the crowd.

4. **Tying up loose ends.** Easy to forget in the commotion of a closing project, but what about any final steps you need to take to wrap the project up fully? It might be a matter of filing correspondence, or dealing with signature pages, or following up on outstanding administration. Whatever it is, keep it on your to-do list until everything is complete. It's worth checking in with your supervisor to ensure that the project actually is complete from your perspective. It's not impossible that there are a few remaining things to be finalised that you've missed.
5. **Acknowledging good work.** Whether it's your own work, or the work of a team member – see if you can spot work done well, and acknowledge it. If it's the work of a senior person, perhaps make a note of anything you could incorporate into your own working style going forwards. If it's your own work, note it down and set a reminder to do the same in future. If it's the work of a junior team member, make sure you thank them for their contribution and leave them with some positive feedback.

Chapter 5

Personal development

In pursuit of that work–life balance

Here's a basic definition of personal development, to begin:

'Personal development covers activities that improve awareness and identity, develop talents and potential, build human capital and facilitate employability, enhance the quality of life and contribute to the realisation of dreams and aspirations.'

Sound good? Let's dive straight in.

The work–life balance

Firstly, what is a 'work–life balance'? In its most obvious form, a work–life balance consists of divisions and boundaries that enable a structured separation of work inside the office, and life outside it. In practice, however, the reality of a work–life balance is fluid and subject to constant evolution. With the development of technology, we're able to take work wherever we want; with the rise of flexible working, we're able to bring our home lives into the traditional working day. With that in mind, here are a few pointers to bear in mind when crafting your own work–life balance.

- **Create your own definitions.** Start by getting clear about what you want. A clear 9-5 division of work from life? An ability to work from home? Flexible hours? Would you be happy to allow work to spill over into your personal life, in return for an ability to do your work away from the office? Your definition of work–life balance will be totally unique to you. Bear in mind, too, that your desires are likely to change over the course of your career.
- **Figure out what's possible.** Look around the office, ask your colleagues, and check the official HR policies. What kind of work–life balance does your office support? Most organisations will have employee wellbeing policies, and these might include flexible hours, or remote working. Make sure you're fully in the know about the official guidelines.
- **Make sure you're equipped.** The work–life balance will only work if you're able to fulfil both objectives: to complete your work to an

excellent standard, and to fulfil your personal objectives for your non-work time. Making sure you have all the equipment to achieve this should be a priority: a reliable, functional laptop; a work phone (if you need one); an up-to-date diary or calendar so that you know where you're meant to be and when. Setting up a space to work from home will also be helpful: dedicate a working area and stick to it (you're likely to be much more productive there than working from the sofa).

- **Review frequently (and adjust accordingly).** Is your life working for you? Aim to check in with yourself frequently about whether your work–life balance is giving you genuine fulfilment (both in a professional and personal capacity). Is it working for your team? For your family? For your mental health? If you can't answer those questions with a resounding 'yes', it's time to review: figure out the issues, work with your team to develop solutions, and experiment with new ways of working. Don't settle: this is your life, after all, and you should make sure the (many) hours that you spend working actually *work* for you.
- **Be here, now.** This is the hardest part of maintaining an effective work–life balance: the art of being fully present with whatever it is you're currently doing. It's an act of mental and intellectual discipline to stay focused, to stay grounded, and to stay with your current activity – whether it's time with friends and family, or time spent on a work assignment.

  Whenever you feel your attention flickering from one thing to another (and yes, it happens to every single one of us), try this: stop the activity completely, take a few seconds to breathe, and remind yourself where you are and what you're trying to do. If you're working, this might mean closing your laptop for a few minutes, or placing your phone face down. If you're at a social event, it might mean excusing yourself for a few minutes to step out and get some air. Give yourself an opportunity to be genuinely present: decide what it is that you need to turn your attention to, and do it. If you're at work, work. If you're not working, be present to whatever it is you *are* doing.

For more on fighting a flighty attention span, see the advice on productivity in **Checklist 5.1**.

Sustainable wellbeing

Again, it might help to start with a general sense of what wellbeing in work actually means. What are we talking about here? For some, workplace wellbeing can mean diversity, mutual respect and a supportive culture. For others, wellbeing might mean a lunchtime yoga class, or getting enough sleep each night. Just like the elusive work–life balance, the concept of wellbeing is subjective: to make sure you're feeling satisfied, you'll need to understand your own priorities. Below we'll cover a few of the basics (but you should continue to make sure they reflect your own components of what it means to create – and maintain – your wellbeing).

- **Get enough sleep**. Seems easy enough, right? However (as you'll probably have discovered if you're a few weeks into the job), it's often easier said than done. Because of its impact on your health, making sure you have enough sleep should probably be one of your main wellbeing priorities. As for the number of hours, everyone is different, but it's generally accepted that most people need at least seven to eight hours of good quality sleep every night.

  If it's a matter of too much work, try and take a step back to analyse the issue. Sleep deficits might be necessary in the short term – for example, if you're working on the closing of a big case or transaction – but don't allow it to become a habit. Set up boundaries with yourself, and stick to them (even if it means skipping your Netflix habit for a few days). You'll be surprised at how many work-related problems are actually easier to deal with after you've had a decent night's sleep. The same applies, of course, to your personal life.
- **Nutrition.** Another basic component of wellbeing is the nutrition you get, and how you get it. Some basic things (that we all obviously know at some level, but can so easily forget, or ignore):

  – Try and take a quick lunch break. Not always possible, of course, but even a walk to get a sandwich can give you a much-needed change in environment (plus, fresh air!). If you can't leave the office, making even a tiny effort to concentrate on your food (look away from your emails for five minutes; eat slowly and with intention) will go a long way.
  – Plan for the day. Knowing what kind of day you'll have (back-to-back meetings? Trips out of the office?) means you can think about when and what you'll eat, and plan for it. If your schedule is packed, make sure you have enough food around so that you can eat regularly and well. Accidentally skipping meals is not particularly helpful for maintaining an energetic, alert mindset throughout the day.
  – Drink enough water. If you're not usually someone who feels thirsty, it can be easy to forget to drink enough during a busy day. The simplest way to stay hydrated (and avoid those awful 5 pm headaches) is to track your intake: fill up a big bottle of water at the start of your day, keep it in sight on your desk, and steadily work your way through it. *Always* take water into long conference calls or meetings. Drinking a good amount of water first thing in the morning can also get you off to a great start.

- **Movement.** Try to get some movement into each day. It doesn't have to be a full gym session or fitness workout. Movement can be as simple as a brisk walk with a podcast, or a stretching session on a yoga mat at home. The key is regularity: get used to being active each day, and you'll soon start to build up a good base level of fitness and flexibility. In the office, make sure you get up enough from your desk. If you have a standing desk, use it. Take the stairs for any office wanderings. Walk to buy your lunch. Get involved with anything your office might offer: morning yoga, lunchtime running clubs, or opportunities to train for charity events – anything that interests you, and (most importantly!) that *feels* good.
- **Posture.** Sit up straight. Good posture will make a huge difference: both in the short-term, and throughout the 80,000 hours(!) that you'll probably spend at a desk over the span of your career. If you need a lesson in good posture, head to a Pilates class for some basic pointers. Your office should also support employees with good quality desk chairs – make sure yours is set up and fitted properly.

Managing productivity

There's a *lot* going on when you first enter the workplace. You're managing new projects, meeting new colleagues and developing a whole range of new skills (not to mention those ongoing attempts to sustain your personal life). It's not unusual to feel overwhelmed by it all: where should you even begin? Productivity 'hacks' are subjective (in other words, they'll only work for you if they fit with your schedule, personality and skillset), but it's worth experimenting with the tools and tips available. In the checklist below, we'll cover a few of the basics.

CHECKLIST 5.1: PRODUCTIVITY

1. **Just one thing.** This is a simple strategy: make sure you know what your top priority is for the day, and don't stop until you're finished with it. The trick with this strategy is to limit yourself to just *one* thing. Don't get overwhelmed, or distracted – just get your single thing out of the way as quickly as possible. The biggest threat to this strategy is a lack of planning: don't allow time to slip away as you try and figure out what your 'thing' is for today. Just spend a few minutes at the end of each evening planning your one thing for the following day, so you'll know what to execute as soon as possible in the morning.
2. **25-minute timers.** This technique – famously known as the Pomodoro technique – breaks your time down into manageable 25-minute segments. Pick a task, set your timer for 25 minutes, and then work – without stopping – for the duration. When the

timer goes off, take a five-minute break, and then start another 25-minute slot. You might even get lost in the flow of the work and decide to skip the five-minute break altogether.

The beauty of this technique is that it strips any procrastination down to its barest form. The question is: can you sit down and work for 25 minutes without your attention span collapsing? Are you disciplined enough? Strong enough? Capable enough? If you like a challenge, this might be the strategy for you.

3. **The 80/20 rule.** Also known as the Pareto principle, this philosophy is based on the idea that 80 per cent of your results come from 20 per cent of your work. The key is to figure out *which* 20 per cent is your winning formula. Feedback and observation will be your greatest assets in this task: watch, listen and ask other people about your work. Figure out which tiny actions are getting you the greatest return – in terms of productivity, success, visibility, or however you choose to measure your professional success. Then, turn your time over to these activities first, with everything else taking a back seat. The key is to keep tracking and observing your inputs and outputs: see what works, see what doesn't, and apportion your time accordingly.
4. **Minding the gaps.** We all have days with gaps: short spaces between appointments, or time waiting for trains, or spare minutes between meetings. What happens to your time during the gaps? The likelihood is that you're flicking open social media, or half-heartedly checking emails. Before you know it, the working day is over, and you're left wondering how the time slipped through your fingers. What could you do to fill the gaps productively?

    - **Eradicate your admin.** Whether you're filing emails, calculating your billable hours, or prioritising your to-do list, it's normally most productive to do this work during periods of 'dead' time between meetings. It doesn't require much mental effort or prior preparation: just jump straight in and see how far you can get in the time available.
    - **Clear your desk.** It might be annoying, but it's incredibly rewarding. Get your desk clear of everything you don't immediately need. Create an effective filing system, and stick to it. Consolidate to-do lists into a single place. Get rid of all the open tabs on your browser, or any irrelevant documents saved to your desktop. You might even find that it helps to deliver clarity and organisation in your work, as well as in your environment!
    - **Plan, organise and prep.** Make sure you know what's coming up in the week ahead (check both work and social appointments, and make sure you don't double-book yourself). Have you scheduled yourself enough time between meetings? Do you have set times to work on your most important projects? Are there any gaps in your week, and how will you fill them? Thinking ahead usually means that you use your time in an effective, powerful way.

5. **Get in the zone.** Just like an athlete, think about preparing a pre-game routine to get you in the mindset for focused periods of work. Making yourself a cup of tea, clearing your desk, putting away your phone – whatever it is, find it and stick to it. Over time, using a pre-work routine will help to psychologically prepare you for a period of focused concentration (which is so often hard to come by during the hectic working week).

Priorities

Priorities: we all have them, but we don't all fully acknowledge them – and so we end up doing the unimportant tasks first, and then stressing about our most crucial pieces of work at the last minute. There are several methods to keep you on track. Let's break them down.

- **Know what your daily priorities are** (you can even subdivide these further into hourly priorities, if that works better for you). Write it down each morning, keep it in your view, and review again at the end of the day before resetting for the following morning.
- **Have a midday check-in.** You can use it as an excuse to pause from your email inbox and have a change of scenery. Recap on what you've achieved so far that day, and make sure your daily priority is still the right one. Are there more important things that have come up during the day that could trigger a realignment?
- **Communicate with your team.** Are your priorities still the right ones, from their perspective? Is there information you should know that would help you stay on track? Are there emails you need to read but that you haven't been copied on? Make it your responsibility to find out.
- If you're working towards a long-term goal, **track your daily priorities over a period of weeks or months.** This should help you to keep an eye on progress and make sure you stick to a consistent path.
- **Use your priorities to determine what you say 'yes' and 'no' to.** This applies as much in work as it does out of it: begin to filter all your commitments through the lens of your main priorities. This one is perhaps the most difficult step, but articulating your priorities to others and having an open discussion about time management will pay significant dividends in the future.

Expectations

That final point leads us straight to the topic of expectations. We're all familiar with the feeling of others' expectations (both in the office and out of it). However, in the working environment, we're mostly concerned with the expectations of those we deliver our work to: the client. Bear in mind, too, that the 'client' here doesn't always have to be an external third party. If you're delivering your work to your supervisor, or to another lawyer or team within your firm, you're working for an internal client. So, how should you manage, meet and exceed their expectations? Here's a step-by-step guide through the process.

CHECKLIST 5.2: MANAGING EXPECTATIONS

1. Start by fully understanding the work. When you're given a task, make sure you know the basics: how long it's expected to take, when the deadline is, what kind of work product you should aim to create, where you should look for further information, etc.
2. Tell the client (who could be your supervisor, in this case) when and what you'll deliver (email analysis? A formal memo? A research project?) and any other contextual information. For your supervisor, 'other contextual information' might include a brief summary of what else you're working on, and how you'll prioritise the work. For an external client, 'other contextual information' might be letting them know that you may have further questions as the task develops, or asking them to provide additional information or documents.
3. When you have an idea of the deadline, figure out if you can set yourself an earlier internal one. Leaving yourself plenty of time will not only take the pressure off (and factor in any nightmare emergency situations), but will also enable you to exceed those expectations in the event you can deliver the work product early. Be careful, though, to make sure you don't rush the work in order to deliver ahead of schedule. Much better to deliver on time and make sure the work is your best.
4. Kick off the work, and keep yourself on track – as far as possible! – with the estimated timeline. The 'priorities' tips above might help to keep you aligned with your deadline.
5. *If* (or – let's face it – *when*) things go slightly off-plan, make sure that everyone stays updated. Communication with your team (including clients) is the solution to most (if not all) deadline drama. Always be looking a couple of steps ahead. If there's anything that might push out the deadline, don't cross your fingers and hope for the best. Do something about it: tell your supervisor; have a discussion; raise the concern with your colleagues. Negotiate a new deadline if you need to, or restructure the project in line with updated expectations. Either way, though, don't struggle through alone.
6. Similarly, if you're realising that you don't know the answer, or you won't reach the outcome the client expects, revise expectations accordingly. When the client is *internal*, take the next opportunity to raise the issue, or schedule in a meeting to discuss (and stick to it). When the client is *external*, speak to your supervisor about how to handle the problem. As above, the key is communication. Presenting your problem along with a proposed solution (one that you've spent some time thinking about) is a helpful approach.

Tailoring your role

Once you start your training contract, you'll soon figure out that there are some things you like, and some things you don't like. To some extent, it's true that you might just have to get on with tasks (and colleagues) that aren't a natural fit for your preferred working style. However, in the longer term, it's possible to think a little more creatively. Welcome to the world of job-tailoring. This is how to do it.

1. **Identify and isolate the aspects of your job that you like the most.** Can you pick out a common thread between them? Perhaps it's a topic or subject; perhaps it's a particular *type* of work that maps perfectly to your strengths and abilities. Whatever it is, notice it – and make a note of it.
2. **Figure out where you can do more of the tasks you love** (this is a much more effective approach than figuring out where you can do less of the tasks you hate). Can you volunteer for specific projects, or offer to supervisor a junior member of the team? Can you make a name for yourself as someone who enjoys *that* particular thing?
3. **Show evidence** – to your supervisor, the team, the client, or the office in general – that you performing more of the tasks you love delivers a net positive benefit to the firm as a whole. Make sure you do the task with excellence, and take every opportunity to learn, grow and improve. Detail and document your evidence whenever you spot it.
4. **Keep your eye on your role as it develops.** It may be, eventually, that your interests and passions shift: make sure you're agile enough in your role to shift with them. Stay interested and keep your eyes open. Try different things. Above all, notice whatever it is that you genuinely enjoy and lean towards that.

Perspective

There are a number of foundational skills you'll need to build during your first few months at work. Obviously, being good at your job is one of them, as well as navigating the change in pace and managing expectations. However, perhaps even more importantly, it's worth investing some time in developing perspective.

With a new group of colleagues, new environment and new timetable, it's easy to slip into the bubble of law firm life. Without even noticing it, you might find yourself adjusting to a new normal. You might start to see your working life (and the working lives of your colleagues) as the *only* way to live. This isn't particularly helpful in the attempt to retain perspective.

Instead, make an active effort to stay tapped in to the outside world. Reach out to friends and family who work elsewhere. Consider taking weekends away from the city in which your office is located. Remind yourself regularly who you are and what your ultimate purpose and goals are about – not just in the context of your work, but in the context of your life in general.

And finally…

A final note on the unique context of life in a law firm. Office life can be difficult at the best of times, but there's often an enhanced pressure in intensely client-focused industries. Anxiety and stress might well be present in your working environment on a regular basis.

It doesn't mean, however, that you have to make it part of your own career trajectory. Stay focused: know why you're in the job and who you're becoming; take care of the basics (get enough sleep, drink enough water, spend enough time outside); check in with yourself regularly. Try to reverse-engineer any moments of stress to figure out what triggered them, and make a note of it.

Ask yourself: how could I navigate this situation differently next time? What can I learn from my own personal reactions, struggles and emotions that might help me improve; become stronger; move forwards? Take ownership of everything you experience. Can you see the difficulties as opportunities to grow?

Finally, remember that you should never have to trudge through difficult times on your own. Build your support systems – both within the office and outside of it – and stay in touch with them. Open, honest communication can often resolve situations that seemed impossible from the inside out. Remember, too, that you form a vital part of others' support systems, even when you're not aware of it.

Chapter 6

Mentors and mentoring

Seeking guidance; giving back

Turns out you can only get so far working on your own: it's time to assemble your team. In this chapter, we'll cover mentors, coaches and sponsors, as well as how to deal with becoming a mentor, coach and supporter for someone else. We'll also look at maintaining, nurturing and developing your mentoring relationship once you've set it up, and how to give the full value-added experience to the people that help you out. After all, what's the point of making it to the top if you haven't built a stellar connection with the people that helped you get there?

Mentors and mentoring

Firstly, the mentor. There's a lot of research out there in favour of the mentoring relationship. The basic view is this: career progression is often a result of opportunities and connections, and those with mentors tend to end up better off. Not only can a great mentor open doors and provide introductions, but they can also be around to supervise your overall development, giving you new ideas and ways of seeing things. But how to find your match?

Finding a mentor

Start with the people you know. Are there any senior people who are already in your circle of connections and who know something about your work or your character? Think creatively: your mentor doesn't have to be someone who works for the same organisation as you. You might find mentors in voluntary roles, or in other positions of responsibility that you've held in the past. Start by listing out everyone that you think might fit the requirements.

If you've run out of options for people you know, try listing out a couple of people you're inspired by, who are also in your immediate network. Perhaps a senior colleague you've encountered in passing, or someone who used to work at your firm. Add these people to your list.

If you're still stuck for ideas, ask around: do you have any peers with great mentoring relationships? Could your supervisor suggest someone, or does your firm have an official mentoring scheme to which you could sign up? Consider other routes, too: perhaps your university alumni organisation offers mentor matching, or other clubs, societies or communities to which you belong might have something similar.

Approaching a mentor

Intimidating, right? Just the thought of approaching a potential target for advice can be enough to put you off the whole project entirely. The key is to be well-prepared: that way, you'll be less likely to feel nervous when approaching your prospective mentor. Follow the steps below and you'll be well on the way to a confident request (and a positive reception).

- **Do more research than you think you'll need.** Start with a basic Google search to find out as much as you can about your prospective mentor. Where did they go to university? What career path have they taken? What are their interests? Do you have anything in common with them? If they've published anything available online, read it – and make sure you have a couple of questions banked about its content.
- **Figure out what you're asking for.** What do you want? Sure, you're hoping that your mentor will help you to figure this out, but you need to start somewhere. Write down a couple of basic career goals that you're hoping your mentor can help you with. Why is this particular person a great match for your dreams and ambitions? What exactly do you want to achieve from the relationship?
- **Plan the details of your approach.** How will you make contact with your mentor? If the person is already in your circle of connections, perhaps you can reach out at a work event or meeting – make sure you have your business card handy, and follow up by email. If you're reaching out to someone you haven't yet met in person, craft your email with care. Make sure it includes enough background about yourself, what you'd like (start with a request for a quick coffee, or a ten-minute chat over the phone), as well as why you admire them (genuine compliments only!).
- **Execute, and follow up.** After you make your initial approach, it might take a while for you and your mentor to get a date in the diary. Be patient: let your mentor lead the way, and work around their requests for times, dates and locations. In the event that one of you cancels last-minute (try and avoid that person being you), make sure you reschedule. Chances are, you only need one good face-to-face meeting to secure the relationship, so make sure you go for it.
- **Demonstrate mentee excellence.** More on adding value in **Checklist 6.1** – for now, just bear in mind that you'll need to demonstrate how

great you are as a potential mentee at the first opportunity. If you manage to get a meeting or call with your mentor locked in, make sure you listen carefully to their advice (and – as always – take notes!). Ask intelligent questions, and discuss how you'll be implementing their guidance. Arrogance, dismissiveness or an inability to receive feedback makes you look like you're not that interested in the mentoring relationship after all – avoid this at all costs.

Mentoring for others

Perhaps you're convinced of the need to have a mentor, but what about the need to *become* a mentor for someone else? Far from being just another thing to add to the to-do list, becoming a mentor for someone else is actually one of the best things you can do to evolve towards greater personal and professional growth.

Why? Well, you'll not only expand and enhance your own network (especially with people who will one day move up to hold more senior positions), but you'll also open yourself up to new perspectives, different ways of thinking and opportunities you hadn't considered. Plus, helping others tends to make you feel good (bonus points).

Finding a mentee

Ok, so you're ready to put some wisdom back in the world – but who should you reach out to? Start small: think about junior people in your own organisation or team who have asked you for help or guidance in the past. Drop them an email; suggest a coffee. Keep it informal, and check in with them about their career-related goals. If there's a way you can help them, offer it. Otherwise, just let them know you're around if they want a sounding board, helping hand or word of advice.

If there's no one in your immediate circle, think about people you might encounter in other capacities. Perhaps you've been involved in open days or vacation schemes, and had a mentoring role that you could cultivate and sustain; perhaps you've worked with paralegals or support staff who have looked to you for help. Again, think creatively – there are bound to be a number of people who regard you as an influence, even if you're not aware of it.

Coaches and coaching

Next up, the coach. Unlike the mentor, your coach is someone who'll be offering specific advice about a particular area for improvement (this is sometimes referred to as 'task-orientated' work). Your coach should give you an opportunity to define – at the outset of the relationship – what it is that you want to achieve or work on. Depending on the type of coach you have, this could be anything from public speaking to promotion prospects; from developing new skills to enhancing old ones. Where mentoring will primarily focus on the *relationship* between you and the mentor over a period of time, coaching will often be *goal-focused, time-limited work.*

Working with a coach

To get the best out of your coach, know exactly what it is that you want. Although part of the coach's role might be to help you discover your true purpose or skillset, knowing yourself before you walk in the room will set you up for a great start. Make sure, too, that you have some way of measuring your own progress (feedback from others? Formal appraisals? Personal perception?) so that you can assess whether the coaching relationship is working for you.

Coaching for others

What about becoming a coach yourself? It's more technical than setting up a mentoring relationship, but – if you have a genuine interest in pursuing coaching alongside your work as a lawyer – it's worth looking into the various study courses available. Becoming a coach for others is a valuable asset to add to your skills portfolio, and might just change the trajectory of someone else's life in the process.

Sponsors and supporters

Finally – and let's take these two categories together – the sponsor and the supporter. These people are not your mentors, and they're not your coaches. They do, however, play a crucial part in setting you up for career success.

Your sponsor is the person who will advocate in your favour, at all the right times and in all the right places. They'll be on your side when it comes to promotion prospects, and will put your name forward when opportunities come up. In short, your sponsor is firmly behind you, and will form an essential step in your career progression (so choose them wisely).

Your supporter plays a similar role to your sponsor, but their presence and advocacy might be a little less visible. Your supporter is likely to be more junior than your sponsor, and may even be a colleague or close friend at your place of work. While your supporter might be putting themselves out there less than your sponsor, they're still an important part of your personal development architecture, and will provide the positive foundations from which your career will accelerate.

Finding sponsors and supporters

It's true that finding sponsors and supporters is harder work than finding mentors. This is because your mentor can stand at a distance from you and your work, offering constructive criticism and handing down wisdom (and the same applies for your coach). Your sponsors and supporters, however, are fully 'with' you, promoting you behind the scenes and openly associating themselves with you. It follows, then, that you're more likely to be noticed and selected by sponsors and supporters, rather than sitting back and letting them come to you.

So, how to get noticed? As well as enhancing your communication skills (**Chapters 1–3**), and figuring out who you are and what you're doing in the world (**Chapters 3** and **8**), there are a number of ways to optimise your chances of ending up with an outstanding team of advocates.

1. Do excellent work, and make sure people know about it. The first point (do excellent work) is somewhat obvious, but the second (make sure people know about it) is a little less so. Perhaps you're not used to broadcasting your achievements, or talking about the things you do well; perhaps you're concerned that it comes across as arrogant or self-absorbed. If that's the case, good news: the subtle art of self-promotion can be done with sensitivity, humility and tact. The bad news, however, is that you'll need to do at least *some* self-elevation if you want to get people to sit up and take notice).
2. Volunteer, get involved and keep your eyes open. Closely related to the idea of promoting your own work is the idea of promoting your personal brand. After **Chapter 3**, you should be feeling a little more confident about your personal brand – if that's the case, get to work on solidifying it by volunteering for opportunities that feel like a good fit.
3. Know where you're going, and let others know as well. Use your feedback meetings (formal and informal) to communicate what you want and where you're headed. Your sponsor will need to know that there's a genuine passion at the heart of their sponsorship project, so make sure you share it. Remember that you don't know where or when your next supporter or sponsor might show up, so it helps to maintain a consistent sense of clarity about your career goals, and to be able to articulate them in any situation that calls for it.

Finding the right people

There's a difference, of course, between gathering a team around you as quickly as you can, and gathering the *right* team around you. As you begin to build your network of mentors, coaches, sponsors and supporters, make sure you ask yourself the important question: is this person the right fit for what I'm trying to achieve?

To break it down a little more, spend some time thinking about the following questions:

- Does this person have the career (or other relevant attributes) that I am inspired by?
- Does this person have a great reputation within my organisation or chosen career field?
- Does this person have the time and resources available to commit to a mentoring, coaching or sponsoring relationship?
- Is this person a good fit in terms of personality, communication and working style?
- Is there anything else that makes me hesitant about entering a mentoring, coaching or sponsoring relationship with this person?

If you have doubts, don't gloss over it – even for the win of getting someone on your team. This applies, in particular, if they're high-profile or well-known: take the time to find a great match for you, rather than jumping in for the prestige or for the ease of it. A good, well-aligned relationship can last the duration of your career: think of it as an investment, and not as something you should rush into.

Personal goal setting

Enough about the other people that will play a part in your career progression: let's get back to you. What about personal goal-setting, objectives and ambitions? Below, you'll find a set of simple structures that can help you map your way through your early career as a lawyer.

In this context, you can think of a 'goal' as an object or aim (in the work context, you might also hear goals referred to as 'performance objectives').

1. The purpose-driven goal-setter

This strategy is for the lawyer who has found their ultimate purpose and knows exactly where they're headed. Purpose-driven goal setting is orientated around a single goal, clearly identified and described with clarity. The task is to work backwards from the overall goal and trace the individual steps needed to get you there (i.e. reverse-engineering the result).

2. The accountability-driven goal-setter

This next strategy is for the lawyer who needs some external pressure. Accountability goal setting is about telling someone what you're planning and where you're headed, and then making sure you check in with them regularly. Ask them to keep you on track, and make sure they're asking you the right questions each time you regroup.

3. The visualisation-led goal-setter

This one is for the dreamers – those with a strong, vivid imagination. Visualisation goal setting relies on you having a vision, and one clear enough to inspire you into action. Visualisers might like to spend time thinking, journalling or working through vision boards in order to get their ideas in order.

4. The acronym-focused goal-setter

You've probably heard this one before: research has indicated that 'SMART' goals (specific, measurable, achievable, relevant and time-based) are more effectively achieved than their vaguer counterparts. If you like the sound of that, and if you love working with templates to define and delimit your goals, the SMART system might be the way forward.

5. The micro-planning goal-setter

This final strategy is for those who adore the details. The micro-focused system works on a day-to-day basis, thinking only about the next immediate step in the system. This will work for you if you like to concentrate on one thing at a time, and if you like your goals to be immediate, practical and actionable.

The art of delegation

So far, we've looked at adding people to your network for the purpose of supporting you through your career on a macro level. Next, let's think about those who will support you through your career on the micro level. More specifically, let's think about the art of delegation.

The components of delegation

A break-down of the components of delegation, to start things off. Delegation is made up of a number of elements:

- the piece of work in question;
- the chain of supervision; and
- the handover, tracking and debriefing processes.

Let's take them step by step.

Firstly, the piece of work in question. Do you know what the task is? As delegator, you'll need to know not only the precise boundaries of the work (how long should it take; what resources are needed; the broader context of the request), but to also understand the content of the task itself. In short, you shouldn't be delegating something you don't fully comprehend yourself. If you don't know how to do the task, take the opportunity to learn – don't pass it off to someone else. This applies even if you think the task is beneath your level of seniority (if it's easy, you should probably know how to do it, right?).

Secondly, the chain of supervision. Who is the ultimate client? Who is your immediate supervisor? Make sure you're familiar with the contours of the chain of seniority: if (as is most likely for junior lawyers) you're in the middle of the chain somewhere, make sure that information flows freely and with clarity between the various team members.

Thirdly, the handover, tracking and debriefing processes. Taking the steps chronologically, you'll need to start with a clear, articulate and comprehensive handover, during which you answer all questions and set appropriate expectations. Next, you'll need to set up a system that allows you to check in on progress as the project develops. Make yourself available for ongoing communication, and schedule in a time for you to call or email to check everything is moving according to plan. Finally, allow plenty of time for debriefing. Once you've received the work product and thoroughly reviewed it, think about what kind of feedback you need to pass on. Make sure you don't skim over this point, either – you'll know from experience (and from **Chapters 3** and **4**) how important feedback can be, so give it the time and space it deserves.

Developing your delegation technique

Once you've got the hang of the basics, and you've had a few chances to test it out with others, think about ways you can upgrade your technique. Here are a few pointers to get you started:

- Can you provide more context to the task? Does your delegate have the background they need to do the job? Do they have the description and narrative needed to make the work interesting? Put yourself in their shoes for a second – would you appreciate knowing a little more about the task to give it some meaning? If so, give them the same treatment.
- Have you suggested a starting point? All good delegation should come with a signpost to the start line. Whether it's a textbook, a website or a precedent, it's good practice (and makes for much more efficient work) if you get the ball rolling by pointing your team member in the right direction.
- Are you ready to take responsibility for the final work product? Regardless of the extent of your delegation, you should always be ready to take full responsibility for the final work product. If there are errors in the work when you pass it on to your own supervisor, they become your

errors (that's what your reviewing process is designed to prevent, after all). Blaming mistakes on someone else looks unprofessional at best (and downright unpleasant at worst).

Chapter 7

Networks and networking

How to expand your circle (and why you should put the effort in)

What's your initial reaction to the word 'networking'? If you're like most people, it probably fills you with a mix of dread and eye-rolling cynicism. Isn't 'networking' just a euphemism for awkward small talk and endless business cards? Is there anything here worth talking about? I think so. In this chapter, we'll break down the true power (and integrity) of networking, as well as setting up some simple steps to take to grow your network without trying too hard (no awkward small talk necessary).

Network development: why bother?

To get where you are right now, on the first steps of the junior lawyer journey, you've probably done your fair share of networking. This makes sense – you need to ensure you stand out at open days and careers fairs, or during vacation schemes or assessment centres. However, doesn't networking lose its purpose once you've successfully negotiated your way into your training contract? Well, no – and this is why not.

- You have no idea – yet – where you'll end up, and what kind of lawyer you might become. Networking will help: by getting to know your colleagues and clients, you'll also tap into their networks (their previous jobs; their experience; their connections). Those networks will be invaluable when it comes to making your own decisions about your work, specialisms and interests.
- You have no idea – yet – who will end up being a potential mentor, coach, sponsor or supporter. For more on the importance of mentors, etc., see **Chapter 6**.
- You'll develop all sorts of skills to add to your portfolio. To name a few: communication, negotiation, collaboration, strategic thinking, and the ability to listen carefully (and respond) to others. You will also make yourself more likeable in the process. Everyone wins.

- You might get a first shot at any new opportunities. If your name is known around the office, you're more likely to be first in line when it comes to new and exciting prospects.
- You'll start to build those essential client-facing skills early on in your career. Because, of course, you're working in a fundamentally client-facing business (and so building up client-networking skills as early as possible can only be a good thing).

The three fundamentals

In this subsection, we'll break it right down. What are the building blocks of the networking professional?

1. Make a plan

Perhaps the thought of planning your network sounds a bit contrived. Fear not: we're not talking about identifying individuals and hunting them down. Instead, this is about giving yourself some general direction. What kind of people do you want in your network? Are you looking for individuals with a specific career focus, or a diversity of background? Is there a particular skill-set you're hoping to benefit from?

To help with structuring your plan, consider making a visual map of your network: start with you in the centre, and then use lines to branch off to people (or groups of people) you'd like to introduce to your network. You don't have to limit yourself to people you already know: be as ambitious as you like, and include people you've heard of, encountered a handful of times, or even unidentified people (i.e. a type of person that you'd like to meet, but haven't yet). Keep your plan updated: refer to it often, and make amendments where necessary.

2. Search for opportunities

When you start to think about it, you'll be surprised at just how many opportunities there are to 'network' during the course of a normal day. Try to think less about organised drinks events, and more of casual conversations in the corridors, or chances to chat amongst colleagues between meetings.

Other frequently overlooked opportunities include the following:

- standing in a queue with someone (think: waiting to get lunch; waiting to use the photocopier; waiting for the lifts);
- before and after conference calls or meetings, if there's an appropriate chance to talk;
- travelling with colleagues anywhere outside the office (external client meetings; seminars; training sessions); and

- any 'extracurricular' activities that your firm might organise outside of working hours (it follows that you should make an effort to get involved in at least a few of these).

3. Be prepared to utilise those opportunities

Do you know who you are and what you're interested in? Do you have your contact details to hand? Can you remember the names of people you meet? Are you skilled in active listening, asking questions and digging deeper? Are you ready to capitalise on networking opportunities whenever they arise, or are you too busy flicking through emails on your phone to notice them?

The real skill is often anticipating when you're about to have a chance to expand your network, and then capitalising on it. The good news is that this skill can be developed, and it is enhanced every time you gain exposure to new networking scenarios.

Maintaining and expanding your network

Let's assume you've got the basics sorted. Once you have the first few people safely within your network, what next? Here's how to keep your network stable, and expand your reach even further.

Network maintenance

- Add the individual names (and contact details, if necessary) to your network plan.
- If you have any detail on the relevant individuals, add that too. Think: likes, dislikes, interests, hobbies, passions, areas of expertise, background information, etc.
- Keep an eye out for things that might interest the individuals in your network. Scan a good-quality news source every day and flag articles, links or blogs that might be of interest. If you do find something relevant, send it over to them, with a short cover note to say hello, and to explain why you thought the item might be worth their time.
- Make notes of any problems or issues that your network members are having, and keep an eye out for potential solutions. If you find something or have an idea that might be relevant, get in touch – again, if appropriate – and mention that you were thinking of them, and have some ideas to help them out. Bear in mind that this one is probably better suited to a call or meeting than email correspondence.
- Can you offer to help the individuals in your network with something? Even if you can't see that they're searching for an obvious solution to a

problem, perhaps you have something to offer. Do you have any specific skills or experience that might be appreciated by others? You can keep it casual: just mention in conversation that you're ready and willing to help out, and you'll almost instantly start to build that sense of connection.

- Even if you don't have anything to share with the individuals in your network, reach out periodically. For closer members of your network, schedule in a regular coffee date (a reminder to yourself to reach out will probably suffice, rather than tying them up to a recurring obligation).
- Think about the personal touch: don't make it look like you copied and pasted from a template. Could you, for example, write a handwritten note? Could you leave a voicemail instead of an email? Could you drop round to see them in person, if they work in the same office as you? Again, the point is not to be annoyingly persistent, but to make sure that (from their perspective) you have a personality, and (from your perspective) that you're building real, human connections.

Network expansion

Look back to your networking plan. Are there people that you'd like to reach out to, but haven't yet – because they're not within your immediate circle of contacts? If so, it's time to expand your network. Here's how:

1. **Step boldly out of your comfort zone.** Change and growth tends to come to the proactive. Can you find ways to step up at work that take you out of your professional comfort zone and into an area of challenge? What about volunteering to host an event for a team or group you're part of, or asking your supervisor if there are any seminars or conferences you can attend? Remind yourself that even if the answer is no, the registration of your interest will be more than enough to make you stand out from the crowd.
2. **Take a long, hard look at your contact list.** Have you been overlooking anyone in your existing contact list that might be worth reconnecting with? Perhaps friends or colleagues you haven't seen in a while? Professors from university or a boss from a previous part-time job? Again, think creatively – you never know where the next career development opportunity is going to come from, so don't limit your search to a specific set of people.
3. **Look out for tiny favours** (and make the most of them). Here's how to avoid networking feeling boring, creepy or pointless: use it to serve others. Can you spot opportunities to do favours – no matter how small – for other people? Building yourself up as someone who is interested, engaged and ready to help is the first step. You'll be staggered at the power of a small favour: people will remember you, be grateful towards

you, and – ultimately – want to return the gesture in some way. These are all helpful building blocks on your way to an enhanced network.

4. **Use social media** – with care and intention. Without diving too deep into the array of social media options out there, let's just go through the basics of networking via the online world.

   - Use a platform with a good reputation. Sounds obvious, but you only have so many hours in a day, and it makes sense to spend them in good-quality online locations. The same applies to the number of platforms you join: don't spread yourself too thinly. Aim for focused effectiveness, not the scattergun approach.
   - Make sure you only post things that you're happy for *everyone* to see. This includes your current boss, your previous boss, and any bosses you might have in the future (as well as, of course, clients, colleagues, friends and family). The internet is a very visible place. Use your discretion.
   - Check the policies of your current firm to see what you can and can't post online. There's usually something that will ask you to distance personal views from your position at the organisation, so make sure you comply with any requirements.

5. **Google yourself**, and act on the results. Regularly run your own name through a search engine. Check the results: are you happy with the picture that they paint? Is there anything you'd rather remove or add? Then, act on it: if there are sites with which you were once affiliated that you'd like taken down, get in touch with the site organisers and make the request. Check back regularly to make sure you know what people will see when they look you up.

   While you're at it, it's worth taking an inventory of all the social media sites on which you have a virtual presence. Are your accounts private, or are you happy for them to be visible? If the latter, are they aligned with your professional brand? Are there any steps you should take to fix the public message you're putting out there?

Effective networking: the basics

In this section, we'll focus on the in-person networking experience. At this stage, we know *why* and *how* to network – but what about when you finally reach that face-to-face meeting? What should you say? How should you say it?

CHECKLIST 7.1: NETWORKING IN PERSON

1. Firstly, ask them their name (and remember it). Seems obvious, but can be easily

overlooked. It's been said that a person's name is the most beautiful sound in the world to them. Use this information to your advantage, and say it to them often.

2. Secondly, tell them your name (first name *and* surname). Not only is this an essential piece of networking engineering so that they can look you up later, but it's also a bonding tool – it lets the two of you speak on a more personal level. Note that saying your full name is generally more memorable than just introducing yourself by first name only.
3. Next, go deeper. Start to build that personal connection, and line up some interesting questions in advance. Bear in mind that most introductory meetings cover the same ground (personal background, career paths, job descriptions) in the same kind of way: can you do anything to make yourself stand out? Can you get the other person talking about their passions, or the things they love about their work? Can you show active listening skills by digging deeper, asking more, and demonstrating genuine curiosity?
4. Once you're in the flow of things, relax. Try not to have a set agenda (thinking only of someone as a potential mentor or connection for your network, for example). Explore the conversation with them without trying too hard to 'achieve' anything. If you feel like you're getting stuck in an interaction, or you're running out of things to contribute to a conversation, just excuse yourself – take a minute to head out of the space, and rejoin a different group on your return.
5. Finally – the practical stuff. Networking events can be lengthy, and often spill over late into the evening. Make sure you've eaten (either beforehand, or early on in the event) and continue to drink water (especially important in the context of an open bar!). If you start to feel like you're losing your focus, leave – probably better to call it a night if you're exhausted, than leave others with a sub-par impression.

The value-added experience

This is where the real work begins. Once you've established, maintained and expanded your network, how can you deliver genuine value for them? What can you do to make yourself important – or, if possible, irreplaceable – in the eyes of your contact list? In this section, we'll break down the 'value-added' experience: what can you deliver that no-one else is offering?

Be a curator

In other words: be someone who collects material of value, and shares it (when appropriate) with targeted members of their network. In terms of material, think about any of the following: articles, podcasts, videos, interviews, events, legal developments, market news, etc. Feel free to add your own ideas and discoveries to the list.

Being a curator demands two things of you. The first is to keep your eyes open and stay aware of what's going on in your field of interest. The second is to select and refine the things you find into a format that is appropriate for sharing with your network.

Let's work with an example to see how this strategy can play out in practice. Take the course of a normal day: it's 8 am, and you're on your way to the office. You know you'll have a long commute (it's rush hour, of course), so you're skimming through relevant email updates and practice news on your phone. You happen to see a news article that mentions some recent activity in the private equity space. From a recent drinks event, you know that a partner in your firm is working to expand their client-base in this department (and even better, you had a quick chat with them about their plans in the area). Bearing this in mind, you email the link to yourself and save it in a folder for later.

Cut to 4 pm that afternoon, and your email traffic is (slightly) slowing down. Perfect timing – flick through your inbox and find that news article. Craft an email to the partner, mentioning that you saw it that morning and remembered your conversation. Add something personal about your own interest (again, keep it genuine and straightforward). If you want to follow up with a request for coffee or a quick meeting, now is your opportunity: tell them you'd love a chance to discuss the topic with them, and ask them if they have a free 15 minutes (keep it short) in the next few weeks. Hit send and – if you're after some kind of response – make a note to yourself to follow up. If you're not looking for a response, just make sure you recorded the correspondence somewhere, so you can bring it up if you have another opportunity to chat to them.

Note that you probably won't receive a response to everything you send. That's to be expected: people are busy, after all. Don't automatically assume they don't value what you wrote, or that they never want to hear from you again. Be politely persistent, continue to deliver value where relevant, and keep at it. You're still enhancing those essential personal development skills, even if you never get a single response.

Be a connector

Take a scan of the people in your network. Can you see patterns? Connections? People you think would get on well, from a business perspective? One way of delivering premium value to the people in your network is to act as an introducer – bringing people together; facilitating new interactions; setting up closer connections. Here are some ideas to get you started:

- **Use an introductory-style email to bring two people together.** Pick two people in your network who have something in common (think beyond the surface level – what about people with similar outlooks, ambitions or characteristics?). Set up a brief introductory email to put them in contact. You don't have to explain why you thought they were a great match, but remember to provide at least some background on each recipient.

Be as complimentary as you like in your introductions – after all, you want them to be interested in each other! Once you've done your work, you can suggest that they drop you off their correspondence (remember to follow up with each of them after some time has passed). Don't set high expectations here: you're not trying to achieve anything other than the satisfaction and service of making the connection.

- **Use networking events as an opportunity to introduce two people.** This is the same set-up as above – but this time, in person. The benefit of this scenario is that your two connected people will be physically forced into establishing a connection (however brief), and will probably be grateful for a helping hand in the networking game.
- **Host or organise your own event, and use the set-up to connect people.** Again, same set-up as above. This time, though, you have the authority to pick and choose connections wherever you spot potential. As the host, it should go without saying that your job involves making guests feel welcomed – it doesn't take much to go a little further and connect people with the intention of strengthening your network.

Be a cultivator

Finally, this category is about cultivating your existing relationships. Even if you don't have additional material to share, or connections to make, can you continue to nurture and deepen the relationships you've established? This is the art of cultivating relationships, and all you need is a simple email template.

CHECKLIST 7.2: NETWORKING EMAIL

1. Kick off your email with an introduction: 'Hi [name of person], I hope you're well. It's been a while since we caught up at [last time you saw them] – I really enjoyed our conversation about [whatever you talked about].'
2. Take it one step deeper with something a little more personal: 'I remember you mentioning you were interested in [anything they brought up]. I'm also interested in [the topic], and have been [thinking/reading/learning] about it in the last few weeks.'
3. If you're hoping for a meeting, insert your request: 'I'd love to get an opportunity to chat to you again about [the topic]. Do you have 15 minutes for a quick coffee some time over the next few weeks?'
4. Wrap up with something open-ended (and not too pushy): 'Either way, it would be great to hear from you. Hope all is well with [insert detail about their work, family background, or any other personal connection you might have developed with them]. Look forward to catching up soon.'

Chapter 8

The bigger picture

Mapping out your future career journey

So, here we are: the final chapter. Finish line in sight. It's time to look to the future – not just your immediate journey as a junior lawyer, but onwards (and upwards, hopefully). In this chapter, we'll cover the skills of strategic planning and career-crafting, as well as the essential mindsets that go along with them.

The unexpected power of thinking ahead

How far ahead should you be thinking in your career? Five-year plan? Ten years? And what are the benefits? Isn't everything going to change along the way in any event? Well, yes – but there's a power to planning ahead that isn't necessarily obvious at first glance. In this section, we'll break down why it's worth your time. The next section will take you through some methods to put it into action.

Why is it worth your time?

1. Mapping the road ahead gives you a sense of purpose

Doing the hard work of figuring out *where* you want to go and *how* you might get there is a deeply revealing process, even if you change everything about your career path as you move through it. Not only will you start to understand your key drivers (i.e. the things you'll need to have in any job in order to stay true to your path), but you'll also begin to understand the vision *behind* the direction you're headed. This kind of information will be invaluable as you make the difficult decisions your career will inevitably throw at you.

2. You're less likely to be caught by surprise

It's true that even the most stable of job markets can shift dramatically, and often with unexpected pace – perhaps the economy takes a turn, or there's a sector shift, or new technology. On a more personal level, you may find yourself in a new set of circumstances that require a change of career. Either way, undertaking consistent career planning will help you to navigate these changes. You'll know what's out there, where you're headed, and what you're looking for – all of which will become your foundations as you set out on an unanticipated path.

3. You'll develop agility in your outlook

Long gone are the days of the 'job for life'. Today's junior lawyers are likely to be fast and flexible with career decisions, and able to pivot when the situation calls for it. Those who frequently practise stepping back to look at the bigger picture will be set up with a significant advantage. The very act of analysing and assessing your own circumstances will make sure you're present in your career, rather than just sleep-walking through it. In turn, this will make sure you're ready to react to the things that come your way. You've been watching your own development, you've planned ahead, and you're ready to move quickly when the time is right.

How to be a strategic planner

Time, then, to start planning. What are the best strategies?

The monthly check-up

Make a date in your calendar for the final day of each month. Take yourself out for coffee somewhere, and reflect on how things have gone, and where things are going. Ask yourself the following questions (and make notes of the answers):

- How well do I feel like the previous month has gone for me?
- How do my achievements/successes in the previous month map into my broader career goals?
- What didn't go so well? How can I use the experience to shape the path ahead?
- Am I happy with my career ambitions, or do I need to tailor them to align with my current situation?
- What's going on in the wider world of work? Are there any significant developments at my firm, in my industry, or in the market as a whole? Can I observe any trends beginning to emerge?
- Have I received any feedback that should be integrated into my career plan? Do I need to ask for any in the next month?
- What are my career goals for next month? Do I need to take any action, or just maintain the work I'm currently doing? Is there anyone I need to talk to, or industries I should research? Where would I like to be next time I sit down for a monthly review?

Your lifelong learning

As a junior lawyer, you're likely to feel frequently challenged. This is, of course, excellent news for your personal development. You might feel, however, that your academic education (in other words, the ability to learn, assimilate and rapidly apply new information) has slowed since you left university. This doesn't have to be the case. You can – and should! – see yourself as a lifelong learner, constantly on the lookout for new ways to enhance your education.

Often, the trouble is that graduating from a structured system of education leaves you in a bit of a void. What should you be learning, and where can you find the information? How can you hold yourself accountable? How do you know which skills and information to pursue? Here are some ideas to get you started:

- Figure out what kind of content will be helpful for you. Perhaps you can see that the senior people in your ideal career all have a similar skill or training; maybe you can already tell – from the nature of the work you're currently doing – what would help you up-level yourself. If you don't know, try asking a mentor or supervisor: what kind of abilities and expertise would help you stand out from the crowd in this profession?
- Next, figure out where you might be able to find the skills, knowledge or training you need. For example, if you know you're headed into a deal-focused department, you might want to refine your ability to negotiate. Or, if you're interested in litigation, skills of advocacy might be your main focus. What kind of training is available? What resources can you get your hands on? Who can you ask for guidance?
- Once you do find a way to enhance your skillset, make sure you continue to hold yourself accountable. Set regular goals and check in with yourself often (use the monthly check-in structure suggested above, if that works for you). Your goals and milestones may need to evolve as you develop and change – refer back to them regularly, and assess them with a critical mindset. If they're not working for you, swap them out for ones that do.

Vision statements and journalling

Ok, the thought of developing a vision statement might seem a bit much, and it's fine if you're not interested in journalling exercises. However, it's worth spending just a little time revisiting the idea. Multiple research studies have come out in favour of regular journalling, and cementing your ambitions through a vision statement can be useful in getting you (and keeping you) on track. In fact, you can integrate aspects of these tools into any strategic planning model that works for you. Here are the basics.

Vision statements

Let's start with what your vision statement is *not*. It is not a collection of hopes and dreams, or a vague gathering of things that inspire you. It also shouldn't be confused with a 'vision board', which is often associated with a collage of pictures representing your ultimate goals. A vision statement isn't any of these things. Instead, it's a declaration of objective: a flexible codification of your core purpose and values. Your vision statement can be anything from a few lines to a few paragraphs, but should accurately and comprehensively capture the direction in which you're headed. Follow the step-by-step guide below to set one up for yourself.

CHECKLIST 8.1: WRITING A VISION STATEMENT

1. Start with a blank sheet of paper and a spare hour in your calendar. Set yourself up properly: minimise distractions, and make sure you have everything you need (previous notes or journals; lists of goals; rough career plans).
2. Figure out your top career goals and your main values. Keep it short: aim for one to three goals, and no more than five values. If you find yourself with an excessively long list, see if you can distil it down with subheadings.
3. Think forward. Keep your attention on the road ahead (five to 10 years in the future should probably be your maximum: you'll get diminishing returns the further you try to predict the future beyond this).
4. Keep your vision statement focused on the positive (i.e. what you *will* achieve, not the inevitable challenges that will come your way). The negatives can – and should! – be thought through ahead of time, but save it for a separate exercise.
5. Make sure you're specific. Vague ideas about purpose and generalised statements of intention are not particularly helpful here: if your vision statement is going to work for you, it needs to use precise language. Re-read the finished article and ask yourself: could I be any clearer? Could I spell it out in greater detail? Is there anything I'd like to say, but have tried to soften with inexact or overcomplicated language? Again, the more honest you can be here, the more effective your statement will become.

Journalling

I know, it's hard to believe, but the simple act of gathering pen, paper and thoughts together can be one of the most effective forms of professional development (and bonus points, it'll cost you pretty much nothing). Here are a few journalling techniques that can help you think about your future, reflect on your past, and accurately record your present.

THE EXPERIENCE LOG

Mark out a couple of pages in your journal to record significant career-related experiences. This could be anything from an interaction that you had with a client or colleague, to a presentation or pitch you gave, or an observation you had about someone else's work. You probably don't need to get too specific about the categorisation: the aim is just to capture the information in a diary-style format, so that you can flick back to it in the future.

One example in which this might be helpful is in preparation for interview – perhaps for an internal opportunity, or for a new job. When it comes to preparing for the inevitable experience-focused questions ('tell me about a time when …'), you'll be ready to go with a bank of examples on hand.

THE WISDOM PAGES

This area of your journal is where you'll carefully gather and record all the pieces of advice that come your way during your early years as a junior lawyer. Make sure you include them in their context, if that's relevant, and attribute them to their author. You can revisit this section periodically to reflect on the advice given, and you may want to elaborate in later pages about the application of any advice that worked for you (or the advice that didn't!).

THE IDENTITY SECTION

These pages can become a personal reflection of who you are (and who people believe you to be) in the context of your work. It might sound a little intense, but it's really just a collection of messages you pick up along the way: compliments, when you receive them; feedback (the good kind and the critical kind); comments about your work and/or your office persona. You can include intentions for how you'd like to shape your personal brand going forwards, as well as your thoughts on the way it's worked out for you so far.

THE DAILY REVIEW

For those of you who would like to develop a regular ritual of reflection, a daily review might be the perfect journalling set-up. Give yourself a set number of questions (about five seems to work well) and try to complete them at the end of each working day. A few suggestions to get you started:

- How would I sum up my working day today?
- What was the highlight? What went well?
- What was the greatest challenge? What can I learn from it?

- What wisdom would I like to take forwards into my day tomorrow?
- What next steps do I need to take now to progress towards my goals?

THE ONE THING CHALLENGE

This final exercise is for those who like the idea of a daily reflection ritual, but who don't want to commit to a full journal entry each day. The 'one thing' challenge enables you to stay on track, keep checking in with yourself, and – best of all – can be done within the space of a few spare minutes. All it requires is a pen, a piece of paper (or even a note on your phone), and two simple questions:

- Today, what was the one thing I did that helped me reach my career goals?
- Tomorrow, what one thing do I need to do to help me reach my career goals?

The trick with this technique is not to do it in isolation (i.e. just filling out each day as it comes and goes): the benefits truly start to kick in when you review the entries from the previous days. Can you see a trend developing? Can you identify times and periods of motivation, periods of procrastination, and the triggers behind them? Can you start to see the patterns developing within your working life? And, finally, can you apply that same insight to set yourself up for enduring, sustainable career success?

Industry trends: where's it all headed?

In this section, we'll look beyond the scope of your personal office life to the wider industry and business of law. Without diving too deep into the detail of legal developments, we'll cover a couple of major trends, and suggest some resources that will help you stay on top of it all. To start with the obvious: the ability to stay on top of this content will be invaluable as your career develops. After all, junior lawyers bear the responsibility for shaping the future of the profession (no pressure). Knowing the context in which you work is, therefore, essential.

Trends to watch out for

Technological disruption

Let's start with the obvious. Long gone are the days where mark-ups were painstakingly done by hand, and faxes were printed out for close review. Technology has already transformed the work of a junior lawyer, and will continue to do so. Things to watch out for (in addition to the absence of a fax machine) are:

- the use of artificial intelligence to do heavy document work (such as due diligence);
- blockchain and cryptocurrencies (the former could have implications for legal document storage and records, amongst other things; the latter could, for example, transform how capital markets work); and
- the shift online for many traditional legal tasks: think e-dispute resolution, virtual mediation, and online client management services (to name just a few examples).

> For more on this, read Richard Susskind's *Tomorrow's Lawyers: An Introduction to Your Future*, 2nd edition (Oxford University Press, 2017).

Portfolio careers

As things shift around us, it's not surprising that the 'job for life' is no longer a key feature of many legal careers. The market choice is broad, the lifespan of a typical career is long, and the ability to walk a path reflecting your unique interests and values has never been greater. Welcome to the era of the portfolio career. Keep your eyes open for developments in flexible working, passion projects and talent diversification.

> For more on this, read Barrie Hopson and Katie Ledger's *And What Do You Do? 10 Steps to Creating a Portfolio Career* (A & C Black Publishers Ltd, 2009).

Globalisation

Following swiftly in the footsteps of digitalisation, yet another change to reshape the structure of a traditional law firm: globalisation. Globalisation (in other words, the international scale and scope of today's businesses) will open up numerous opportunities: not only the ability to take an overseas secondment (if your firm offers it), but the chance to interact with global teams in the course of your everyday work. Watch out for developments on the international level, too – it's possible that the overarching legal frameworks of tomorrow may come from international bodies, rather than national governments.

> For more on this, read James Bacchus' *The Willing World: Shaping and Sharing a Sustainable Global Prosperity* (Cambridge University Press, 2018).

Alternative business structures

We're not just talking about the new legal structures of businesses here (although these are certainly changes to keep an eye on, too). Under the heading of 'alternative business structures', you're likely to see a lot of things developing in the next few years: new ways of billing clients, evolution in firm hierarchies, new positions and opportunities as lawyers (both within client facing roles and elsewhere). Watch the market – not just your own firm, but the firms of your friends and peers elsewhere in the profession – to see where things might be headed.

> For more on this, read Charles D. Ellis' *What It Takes: Seven Secrets of Success from the World's Greatest Professional Firms* (John Wiley & Sons, 2013).

The essential mindset tools

In this final section, we'll cover the mindset tools that are crucial for sustainable success in the legal profession. As you commence your strategic planning, don't forget the most important aspect (and the common underlying theme): you and your personal foundations for a long, successful career. Here are the basics you'll want to work on, and some tips for developing them.

Agility

Agility: the ability to move quickly and easily. This skill will – obviously – be essential in a rapidly changing industry, in which you'll be required to pivot and reinvent and reimagine at regular intervals. The ability to walk lightly; to be able to shape and form your identity as you move through your career; to be awake and aware to the transformations around you – these abilities will be essential for success.

Resilience

Resilience: the capacity to recover quickly from difficulties. Your career path is long, and will be paved with all of the mistakes, errors and missteps you make along the way (as well as the positive stuff, of course!). When it comes to resilience, the mistakes themselves are irrelevant: it's your response to the mistakes that matters. What will you create out of your career? How will you allow errors to form your future decisions?

Resilience is about taking the things that happen to you – good and bad – and using them as an opportunity to learn, grow and move forward. How will you choose to respond?

Perspective

Perspective: a point of view; a way of considering things. Your perspective is the way you choose to view the world. It's the ability to zoom out of the minutiae and see the bigger picture. It's a choice to step back, reflect, and decide – with clarity – the things that matter (and the things that don't).

Perspective will be essential on your journey to future career success. Not only will it enable you to see the bigger picture at a time when others are enmeshed in the details, but it will also help to foster a sense of wellbeing, clarity and peace. There is an immense power for you here: the ability to know what's important, be clear on your priorities, and stay firmly on your path.

Chapter 9

Expert advice

Learn from the professionals

Time to hear it from the experts. In this chapter, we'll work through your most frequently asked questions, and get the low-down from those who've already worked through them successfully. Dive straight in, or flick through the questions to find those most relevant to you right now – enjoy!

Q. Let's talk about the transition from student to professional. What was the most difficult part of that transition? How did you overcome it?

> 'I think the biggest challenge was the nature of the work. In an academic setting, the work is usually quite controlled – you get the sense of what the examiner is looking for in the question, as it's set out. When you're in a professional setting, the problems you're solving are rarely contained! Most likely, you'll be dealing with a multitude of practical, commercial and technical questions. Solving the issue will need not only technical ability but a genuine understanding of the client's business and context. This is why there's so much emphasis on "commercial awareness" during the assessment process – it really does matter!'
>
> *Emily – junior lawyer; city firm*

> 'For me, it was a matter of adjusting to a new environment. Being in the workplace comes with so many new conventions and ways of behaving – it takes a while to adjust! I think my best strategy was to watch and learn – I spent the first few months listening much more than talking. I wanted to pick up on how the senior people behaved in the business, and then model my own habits and ways of working around that.'
>
> *Jacob – junior lawyer; regional practice*

> 'In the beginning, part of the challenge was the really basic things: managing my wellbeing, making sure I got enough sleep, making sure my workload didn't feel overwhelming or out of hand. When you step out of an academic environment, you lose a bit of the autonomy you might have had to structure your time in the way that works best for you. Your day is suddenly shaped by the client and by your supervisors, and it takes a bit of getting used to! There's a lot to be learned – not just the technical part of the job, but also about managing your energy, stress levels and general sense of balance. It's hard to remember during your first few months, but there's a long way to go in your legal career – so make sure you take care of yourself on the journey!'
>
> *Rosie – trainee lawyer; city firm*

'The new terminology! When I started my first seat, I felt like everyone was speaking a different language. In some areas of practice, the jargon is so heavy that it's difficult to understand what people are talking about most of the time, and sometimes I worried about bothering my supervisor with constant questions and clarifications. If you're in the same position: firstly, don't worry – you'll get used to the new lexicon sooner than you think; and secondly, don't be afraid to ask! A well-timed, carefully constructed question is usually welcomed. In fact, it's the junior lawyers who are confident enough to ask the questions that stand out (in a good way!) from everyone else.'

Maria – junior lawyer; regional firm

'It wasn't just one particular thing for me – it was the combination of everything! The new offices, the commute, the new colleagues, new concepts and things to understand, new routines … it can all seem a bit much at once! It's an exciting time, however – as much as it seems daunting at first, you'll look back at the transitional period as a time of incredible growth and change. Keep your eyes open, take lots of notes, ask as many questions as possible, and enjoy it – before you know it, you'll be settled in and feeling like you've been there forever!'

Christopher – mid-level associate; high street firm

'Above all, the most difficult part of the transition was dealing with the absence of structure in my new job. When you're at university, someone else is responsible for your learning and development. You just have to show up, do the work well, and take the exam at the end of the year! But when you start work, no one is taking overall responsibility for your own career progression and personal development. You have to step up and start to craft your own career path – and it's hard work! It usually means a lot of reflection, enough motivation and discipline to keep checking in with yourself, and a good team of mentors/supervisors to keep you on track.

Relatedly, the other thing is not having a pre-planned structure to your year. There are no set "term dates" – you have to decide for yourself when to take leave, and what your year will look like as you move through it. Again, it requires quite a bit of intentional planning: to really make the most of it, you have to discipline yourself into thinking ahead. It's worth it, however – building a structure around your working life will be one of the most valuable things you can do for your professional and personal wellbeing.'

Adam – trainee lawyer; city firm

'There were two main things I found difficult when transitioning from university to professional life. The first was the change in pace. When I was a student, I had almost complete control over the time I took to complete tasks: I would have a deadline, but these were essay deadlines or exam dates, giving me far more preparation time than you ever expect to see in the workplace, and I generally had fewer things to juggle. In the workplace, I had to learn to work faster on multiple different pieces of work, all while not sacrificing the quality of the work.

That leads into the second thing (which I was repeatedly warned would be a challenge but didn't fully appreciate until I began work), which is how terrible you feel like you're doing in the early days. At university I would pour hours into an essay, and get feedback, but never be expected to do it again, and rarely got it completely wrong. But your attitude towards success needs to change at work, and you have to learn to accept a different form of criticism and a different approach to learning from past mistakes. You're not stupid for getting things wrong in the early days, and you pick things up surprisingly fast.'

Georgina – trainee lawyer; city firm

Q. What about your biggest challenge as a junior lawyer? How did you navigate it? What did it teach you?

'My biggest challenge was learning to manage expectations. I am always too fast to accept work on a deadline I know won't be possible. My most stressful times have been when I've given too many people unrealistic time frames and ended up either letting people down or delivering work I know is substandard. Learning to prioritise and communicate properly was a real challenge early on, but has made a huge difference.'

Georgina – trainee lawyer; city firm

'Setting my own expectations too high! I put a lot of unrealistic pressure on myself when entering the workplace. But your career isn't a sprint, it's a long path, and you need to pace yourself. It's not like a university term, where you can see the end of the road before you even get started. Take things slowly, don't overcommit, let yourself make mistakes – and above all, go easy on yourself. It's a massive advantage to your own personal and professional development if you can cultivate some compassion for yourself along the way.'

Adam – trainee lawyer; city firm

'The most significant challenge was not understanding how to communicate properly. So many times, a simple misunderstanding or miscommunication was escalated into an actual problem because I didn't speak to someone about it at the first opportunity. Most serious professional errors can be avoided if you keep the channels of communication clear and open. Don't be afraid to speak up if you think there's something to discuss with a supervisor – you're not a burden on their time; that's what they're there for! It will make all the difference: you'll get another opinion on your work or another perspective on your situation, and they get the satisfaction of knowing that you're on the right track.'

Emily – junior lawyer; city firm

'I'd be lying if I said that the hours weren't hard! However, in all honesty, long hours weren't the biggest challenge. Most firms are conscious of the need for juniors to have some kind of work–life balance, and supervisors are often keeping an eye on your hours and workload to make sure you're doing OK. Instead, the biggest thing for me was actually making the most of the time I had out of the office. Worrying about work, or feeling stressed or anxious about the week ahead is not the most productive way to spend your weekend. Easier said than done, of course, but try to maintain the habits and practices that make you feel more balanced and rested. It could be seeing friends, or catching up with family – or perhaps even spending some time alone with a decent book, or taking a long walk. Whatever it is that feeds your soul on your days off: find it, and don't lose sight of it.'

Andrew – mid-level associate; high street firm

'Without a doubt, it was being introduced to working in a team. Sounds obvious, but I'd never done the majority of my professional work in a team structure before! At university, you're always working for yourself and with yourself, and you're marked against the other students at the end of the year (so they are, in a sense, your competitors).

In the working environment, you're suddenly part of a much larger structure, working towards a much larger goal. You need to think not only about the expectations of those above you, but also those below you – I always forgot that I needed to manage the time of paralegals and other juniors working on matters with me! It requires you to step outside your own structure and concerns, and start to focus on those around you: what kind of time management and planning would be best for the team? What does your supervisor need to know about the project that you haven't yet discussed with them? How can you best facilitate communication and open discussion between team members (and with the client)? It all takes a bit of getting used to.

It taught me a lot – not just about myself (and my ability to work well with others), but also about the importance of seeing and communicating the overall purpose of a project. To keep a team motivated, you can't just have a personal mission. It needs to be driven and inspired by the overarching team vision – perhaps it's to deliver an excellent piece of work for a particular client, or to produce a piece of published material to make the firm stand out from its competitors. Whatever it is, make sure the whole team knows it, and stands behind it. It's much more effective to lead with purpose, rather than personal initiative.'

Stephen – senior associate; high street firm

Q. If there was one piece of advice you could hand down to the next generation of junior lawyers, what would it be?

'Don't obsess over past mistakes. Take criticism, or constructive feedback, and use it going forward – but don't get bogged down in going over what went wrong. It will just make you miserable.'

Georgina – trainee lawyer; city firm

'Keep up to date with what the market is doing, and what the latest trends are in the legal world. So many junior lawyers just keep their heads down, getting on with whatever is right in front of them – but you can easily raise the bar by taking a look around and checking out where the industry is headed in the future. Even taking a few minutes every day to scan the legal news and any particular updates relevant to your area of practice will put you ahead of the game.

Take any opportunities that arise to get involved in new and developing areas of law. Ask if you can go along to conferences or talks that sound interesting. Make yourself the go-to person for new legal developments in your particular field of expertise. It sounds like a lot, but you start slowly – build it up, and see where it takes you. The effort compounds, and you'll be amazed at where you might end up!'

Simon – mid-level associate; city firm

'Develop the skills that will be most essential to you as the legal world becomes more automated. Things like emotional intelligence, strategic planning, creative problem-solving, negotiation … these will be the essential skills. Due diligence and heavily document-focused work will (and already does) carry less importance when it comes to the law firm of the future.

One other thing: stay on top of your own professional development. No one else will do it for you!'

Emily – junior lawyer; city firm

'Get enough sleep! Seriously. So many errors of judgment, mixed messages and miscommunications are the result of not having enough sleep over a long period of time. Even if work pressures demand a couple of late nights in a row, make sure you compensate yourself for it properly. Learn how much sleep you need to function at your best, and make it a clear boundary for yourself. No point doing your job if you're not able to demonstrate your full potential because you're half-asleep!'

Christopher – mid-level associate; high street firm

'Ask more questions. Sounds simple, but it's so effective. Trainees and junior lawyers who ask a lot of intelligent questions are the ones that get trusted with the responsibility – because the senior lawyers know that they've taken time to really get to grips with the matter. Asking questions is one of the best ways to rapidly expand your scope of knowledge. What better way to find out the answer to a tricky question than to ask someone who's done it a hundred times before?

There's an art to asking questions, of course – as with anything, you need to time it right, and make sure that you've done the appropriate research beforehand. In other words, it shouldn't be used as a short-cut to having to do the work yourself. But – if used in the right way – asking questions is your guaranteed route to professional success.'

William – partner; city firm

Q. If you could do your time as a junior lawyer again, what (if anything) would you have done differently?

'I really let my health decline in my first year: I just didn't look after myself, and stopped thinking about exercise, nutrition and sleep patterns. That was really unnecessary – even at the busiest times I could have easily taken better care of myself, and I wish I had. Now, I try to make sure I don't fall into that mindset again.'

Emily – junior lawyer; city firm

'I would have listened much more! When I was starting out, I was so keen to get involved in the work that I spent too much time diving into projects and not enough time observing, listening and picking up wisdom from other people. I think I also should have worked on my personal development more. The first few months were such a whirlwind that I didn't feel I had the time to properly reflect on my progress. In hindsight, I should have made that a priority.'

Andrew – mid-level associate; high street firm

'I held myself back in a lot of ways because I didn't have the confidence to step up and let people know I was capable. I often doubted my own abilities when, in fact, I was perfectly aware of how to do the work to a high standard. I wish I had trusted my instincts more, put myself forward more often and generally just made myself heard!'

Sophie – senior associate; city firm

'I think I should have spent more time building networks and relationships with other people within the firm. As a junior lawyer, you're often perfectly placed on a deal to integrate yourself in the wider team – you get exposure to all levels of the team, and often end up working with people from different departments or offices. I should have taken the opportunity to set the foundations for the networks I wanted to build in the future. Start early, and the interest on your investment will compound …'

Christopher – mid-level associate; high street firm

'More perspective. Things that seemed so important back then – a typo; a miscommunication; an awkward phone call! – seem completely insignificant now. It's hard to retain a sense of perspective when you're so junior, because you literally don't know any different – after all, you don't have any other experiences as a basis for comparison! However, as you begin to move through your career, it won't take long for you to develop a broader perspective of what it means to succeed – a longer-term view of things. I suppose it's not something you can do immediately, but I would have benefitted from keeping it in mind, even in those first few months. Mistakes are usually fixable, decisions are usually not permanent, and you should let yourself take a broader viewpoint of it all!'

William – partner; city firm

'Take ownership! I would have stood behind every piece of work with confidence – because, honestly, I had done my best using the experience and information I had. Instead, I often felt cautious or doubted myself when it came to reviewing my own work. A lot of the time, good work that I'd helped with was attributed to someone else's credit, just because they were able to speak up and claim it. I'm not saying I've completely conquered this one – I'm still working on speaking up to promote my own work – but I'm definitely working on it.'

Paul – associate; regional firm

Q. What about your networks? Where did you find support during the transition into professional life?

'I turned to slightly more senior lawyers for advice. Really senior lawyers and partners are an invaluable source of legal information and inspiration, but I found that people just a couple of years ahead of me in their career were the best ones to turn for when I needed advice. They could remember what it was like in my position, but had got through it and found ways of handling the situations I was struggling with.'

Georgina – trainee lawyer; city firm

'One thing I did that seemed to be particularly effective was attempt to build networks everywhere – not only with supervisors and more senior people on every project, but also with paralegals, support staff, administrative staff, and the team on reception. As I became an associate, and moved further up the structure of seniority, these relationships became invaluable to me on a personal level, as well as a professional level. I felt like I was fully integrated into my firm, and it gave me a sense of purpose and belonging as I continued my career.'

Christopher – mid-level associate; high street firm

'In my first couple of months, I said yes to everything – all networking events, all firm-organised drinks, all talks, debates and panel discussions. I wanted to get involved and meet as many people as I could, right from the start! While I wouldn't necessarily recommend that approach in the long term (you would burn out pretty quickly, I'd imagine), it was incredibly helpful in those initial stages of network building. I met so many new people, and some of those relationships have lasted long into my career. I guess my advice is to capitalise on that "new starter" energy – throw yourself in, make the most of every opportunity, and enjoy it!'

Andrew – mid-level associate; high street firm

'I actually found a lot of support in friends who'd gone into the city in other law firms – or even in other jobs entirely. A lot of people will be working similar hours, in similar client-driven industries, and catching up with them to get their advice and hear their experiences was always helpful. It also made me feel part of a broader community of junior professionals. And it works both ways, of course – don't forget that you form a vital part of their network-building and professional development ...'

Amelia – mid-level associate; high street firm

Q. What was the most valuable piece of advice you received yourself?

'Practise what you're about to say before you pick up the phone. People probably don't consider this one because it sounds so obvious, but seriously – the amount of awkward introductions I've had with trainees from various firms is massive. Just know what you're going to say to start, the essential information you want to convey, and how you're going to end the call – before you start talking to the other person. Make notes if you have to! It doesn't matter if you feel stupid. Better than making the other person wonder if you've called them by accident as you meander through a monologue ...'

Amelia – mid-level associate; high street firm

'Proof-read your emails! Not just once, but twice ...'

Georgina – trainee lawyer; city firm

'Make the effort to know who everyone is. I went to a vacation scheme dinner once where a partner mistakenly thought one of his own trainees was a vacation scheme student. Just don't do it. It's disrespectful – and it makes you look like you don't care.'

Rosie – trainee lawyer; city firm

'Ask questions. If they're sensible, and you've done your basic research, just ask – it will often shortcut things for you by a significant degree, and save the client a lot of billable time in the process. You're not supposed to know everything! You're just starting out. Let yourself be a student.'

William – partner; city firm

'Get the basics right before you worry about impressing people. Typos, miscommunications, poor formatting, unanswered emails – these things might seem tiny, but a pattern of behaviour will create a reputation of carelessness. I'm not saying it's fair, but it's just better to be on the other side of that assumption! At least with your work free of basic mistakes, you can start to build that reputation of excellence that you deserve.'

Jonathan – trainee lawyer; city firm

'Don't make any dramatic decisions when you haven't had enough sleep, or enough time away from your screen. If you're super time-pressured, make sure you run it past someone else. If you can, step away from the office! Get some fresh air, and/or a good night's sleep, and revisit the thing in the morning.'

Sam – trainee lawyer; regional firm

'Take notes, and actually review them when you have the time! It might sound like obvious advice, but the only effective way you're going to advance your own development is to tutor yourself as if you were still in university. That means, in practical terms, taking notes when you learn something new. It means returning to those notes when you have time and even scheduling in some personal development time into your own diary. It also means revising those notes – assimilating them into your practical experience as a lawyer, so you don't end up making the same mistake twice. Yes, it's a long and difficult process – that's why not everyone does it – and the results aren't an immediate, linear pay-off. Personal and professional growth is a long process, and the results can seem almost imperceptible at first. However, a sustained period of observing, reflecting and reviewing will set you up for success. The kind of success you'll get with this process won't just be a quick-fix, short-term solution; it will be the foundations of your future career.'

Salma – senior associate; regional firm

Q. How do you manage your wellbeing as a junior lawyer? Any tips?

'I have friends who don't work in the city, and speaking to them has been a really useful way of keeping my wellbeing in mind, as they haven't become desensitised to the high levels of stress and low levels of self-care that other people who work in similar jobs sometimes view as normal. My top tip would be to talk about things other than work as frequently as possible, even if just to be able to tell when you're obsessing over it and maybe need to address that.'

Emily – junior lawyer; city firm

'Figure out what your boundaries are – the things you need to do regularly to make sure you stay well – and stick to them. Boundaries will be different for everyone, and will depend on your personal circumstances as well as your non-work commitments. However, invest some time in working through them, and begin to create a sense of work–life balance for yourself (don't wait for someone to hand it to you!).

For example, a boundary might look like trying to have a work-free evening every week to spend with a partner or close friend. Making the commitment to yourself will help you stick to it – and, of course, it doesn't need to involve someone else! Maybe your boundaries are as simple as getting to the gym a certain number of times every week, or spending a lunchbreak out of the office. Experiment: see what makes you feel good, and then integrate it into your everyday working life.'

Christopher – mid-level associate; high street firm

'Kill your notifications! This is so easy to do, and will drastically change your life. You don't have to switch up the regularity with which you check emails, but just try turning off the noise or pop-ups on your phone or laptop, and see what happens. It's often the case that the notification noise or image triggers an immediate response in you – it instantly makes you more stressed, more distracted and more reactive. This is not the state in which you want to respond to a professional email! Taking the triggers away will let you come into control of your inbox – you choose when to look, and the influx of correspondence is under your authority (not the other way round …).'

Daniel – junior lawyer; city firm

'I think the little things are really powerful. The small habits and routines that make up your day can either set you up for long-term success, or not – choose them carefully. Even things like making sure to take a regular lunch-break to walk outside, or doing at least one activity every day that keeps you grounded and happy – these are the things that make a difference over time.

In practical terms, the first step might be to take an inventory of all the things you do during the day. What little habits can you spot that might make a difference to your wellbeing – either in a positive or negative way? Can you identify patterns that might add up to cause certain emotions or consequences? If you know there are things in your life that make you feel good (exercising, for example, or calling your family regularly), schedule them in. Be disciplined about it, even if it feels pointless. Hold yourself accountable. Think about journalling or other self-reflection techniques so you can see what works (and then do more of it).

The other thing to watch is how you react during busy periods at work. Are there habits that you automatically let slide? Is it possible to catch yourself when you feel the tendency to give into workload overwhelm, and instead, step back, give yourself some space and reassess the situation?

If there's one thing I've learned about busy periods, it's that they're nearly always exacerbated by your own stress and anxiety. When you take the time to look at the situation objectively, and with the benefit of some space and self-reflection, you'll usually see that things are nowhere near as intimidatingly awful as they first appeared.'

Stephen – senior associate; high street firm

Q. What one thing would have made the transition into professional life easier for you?

'A mentor. I finally got myself a mentor in my second year as a trainee, but I know they would have made that initial transition so much easier, if I'd had the guidance at that point. My advice would be not to wait for a mentor to land in your life, as if by magic. Search them out. Be methodical and intentional. Know what kind of support you want, and what kind of person would be best to provide it. Do your research, prepare your questions, and set out to find your team.'

Rosie – trainee lawyer; city firm

'A better relationship with my supervisor. I wish I'd had the confidence to ask them for more feedback, instead of feeling like I was constantly bothering them. It goes both ways: you need to ask for what you want – don't assume they can read your mind. Later in my career, I started asking for and receiving regular feedback from the people I worked with – and it made dramatic differences in my work (and in my self-confidence!).'

Andrew – mid-level associate, high street firm

'More interactions with the lawyers in the intake just before my own. Even though some of them were only six months ahead of where I was, most of the issues I was having were common to trainees as a whole. I only discovered this after mentoring a first seat trainee myself, and realising that I'd been through an incredibly similar journey in my own training contract, and had encountered many of the same mistakes. Talking to someone just a couple of steps ahead of you on the path can be one of the most helpful things to ease the transition into professional life.'

Emily – junior lawyer; city firm

Chapter 10

A final thought

To be honest, this wasn't really where I thought I'd end up. I grew up on the 19th floor of a council estate in East London, without any understanding of what 'people in the city' do. It's not that my journey into law was any harder than others, but I often felt like I was starting from nowhere, with no visibility or background knowledge of the journey ahead. It's one of the reasons that writing this book was so important to me: to set out the basics so that other new lawyers – from whatever background – can get themselves up to speed as fast as possible.

There's a lot of work to be done in widening access to employment, but there are also some great organisations doing important work, right now. One of those organisations is Young Women's Trust, and I'm donating an amount of the proceeds from this book towards their programmes and outreach activities. There's some detail about their work below, but for more information, check out their website (**www.youngwomenstrust.org**).

Young Women's Trust

Young Women's Trust supports young women aged 18–30, especially those struggling to live on low or no pay, to get into work that is right for them. Having been originally founded over 150 years ago as YWCA England and Wales, Young Women's Trust believes that all young women should have the opportunity to work and thrive. The charity offers free coaching and personalised advice on job applications, conducts research, runs campaigns and works with young women to build confidence and advocate for fair financial futures.

Appendix A

Mapping your personal brand

1. Your strengths

Let's start with your strengths. Think back to a time in the past where you've received great feedback for a piece of work or a project. What was it, in particular, that you were being congratulated on? Your writing style? Your commercial awareness? Your organisational skills? Note down anything that seems relevant – and pay particular attention to anything that aligns with other pieces of feedback you've received.

2. Your best work

Next, recall a piece of work or project that you felt great about – one that tapped into all of your abilities and challenged you to produce a successful outcome. What was it about the work that you enjoyed? Get specific: was it the nature of the work itself? The topic you were dealing with? The team you worked alongside? Make a note of anything you pick up.

3. Your purpose and passions

Think about your purpose and passions. (The two will often come together: it might be the case that you discover your passions as you pursue a greater purpose, or vice versa.)

If you're not sure you've found your purpose or passion yet, consider the following:

- **What do you want?** Make a list of everything that comes to mind (and be honest). Then go one step deeper. If you've noted down that you want career success, or a bigger salary, ask yourself: what kind of success do I want? Why do I want it? When would a certain salary be enough? Keep asking until you end up with a list full of specific, identifiable items.
- **What gets you up in the morning?** We all have a reason to keep going – even if it's buried somewhere deep down. Is it family? Community? A sense of curiosity about the world? Again, get specific – and be honest.
- **Which challenges in the world get you most passionate?** Politics? Inequality? Justice? Is there an issue that makes you want to stand up and do something about it? Is there a cause that needs to be fought for? A problem that needs to be solved? Something – or someone – that needs your help?

Look back through your answers to these questions, and identify common threads. Maybe there's a theme developing (don't worry if there isn't – just experiment with searching for connections). Maybe you're realising that there's way more to be passionate about than you previously thought.

4. Your story

Track your story – from the very beginning, all the way to the current moment. Make particular notes of the following:

- any childhood experiences that shape the way you see the world;
- any mentors, guides or teachers that opened your eyes to something; and
- places in which you lived or worked that showed you a new culture, or a new way of life, or a new community.

How did these experiences change you? How do you see things differently now? How did you choose to respond to things that happened to you?

5. Your future

Develop your story. What kind of personal brand do you want to take into your future? Can you think of people whose personal brands inspire you? How can you walk towards this as your career develops?

6. An integrated path

Final step: draw all of the threads together. Working back through your answers to the previous questions, look for common themes and overarching connections. Is there an area where your skills and abilities match up to the things you're most passionate about? Are there any similarities between the formative experiences of your life and the work you feel compelled to do in the world?

Appendix B

'Cheat sheet': a template

TOPIC:	
DATE:	
1. A brief summary of the topic/subject:	
2. Most important things to remember:	
3. Experiences of the topic/subject in practice:	
4. Things to watch out for/common mistakes:	
5. Top tips and advice for dealing with the topic/subject:	
Other notes, thoughts and observations...	

Index